First Corinthians

The Expositor's Bible Study and Commentary

DR. MAXWELL SHIMBA

Shimba Publishing LLC

Printed in the United States of America

First Printing Edition 2023

SHIMBA
PUBLISHING

Table of Contents

About First Corinthians

The Book of 1 Corinthians, as well as the Book of 2 Corinthians, is believed to have been written by the Apostle Paul in the mid-50s AD. Scholars generally date 1 Corinthians to around 54-55 AD and 2 Corinthians to 55-56 AD. These dates are approximate, and there may be some variations in dating among scholars, but these letters were composed during the middle of the first century, making them among the earliest Christian writings.

In the First Epistle to the Corinthians (1 Corinthians), the Apostle Paul was addressing the Christian community in the city of Corinth. He wrote this letter to address a variety of issues and concerns that were affecting the Corinthian church. Some of the key reasons for writing this letter include:

1. Division and Strife: The Corinthian church was experiencing divisions and quarrels. Members were aligning themselves with different leaders, such as Paul, Apollos, and Cephas (Peter), which led to factions and conflicts within the church. Paul sought to address these divisions and promote unity among believers.

2. Immorality: There were reports of sexual immorality within the Corinthian church, including a specific case of incest. Paul provided moral guidance and instructions on how to deal with these issues within the Christian community.

3. Lawsuits among Believers: Paul addressed the problem of believers taking legal action against one another in the secular courts, which he considered a poor witness for the faith. He encouraged them to resolve their disputes within the church.

4. Questions about Marriage and Divorce: The Corinthians had questions about marriage, divorce, and the status of believers married to unbelievers. Paul provided guidance on these matters.

5. Meat Offered to Idols: The Corinthians inquired about whether it was acceptable to eat meat that had been offered to idols. Paul offered instruction on this issue, emphasizing the importance of not causing a weaker brother to stumble.

6. Spiritual Gifts: The Corinthians were experiencing spiritual gifts but were using them in a disorderly manner during their gatherings. Paul provided guidance on the proper use of spiritual gifts and the importance of love in all Christian activities.

7. The Resurrection of the Dead: There were some doubts and misunderstandings regarding the resurrection of the dead among the Corinthians. Paul addressed these concerns and affirmed the resurrection as a central Christian belief.

Throughout the letter, Paul's central message is to promote unity, godly living, and love among the believers in Corinth. He draws upon his authority as an apostle to instruct and guide them in matters of faith, conduct, and doctrine.

The First Corinthians serves as a valuable resource for understanding the challenges and issues facing early Christian communities and how the apostolic leadership sought to address them through the guidance of the Holy Spirit.

Unity and Wisdom in Christ

The theme of 1 Corinthians chapter 1 is "Unity and Wisdom in Christ." In this chapter, the Apostle Paul addresses the issue of division and discord within the Corinthian church. He emphasizes the importance of unity among believers and the ultimate wisdom found in Christ. Here's an overview of the main themes and points in 1 Corinthians chapter 1:

1. Unity and No Divisions (1 Corinthians 1:10-17): Paul begins by addressing the issue of division and factionalism in the church. He pleads with the Corinthians to be united in mind and judgment and to avoid quarreling and divisions. He stresses that the focus should be on preaching the gospel, not on personalities or human wisdom.

2. The Wisdom of the Cross (1 Corinthians 1:18-25): Paul contrasts the message of the cross with human wisdom and philosophy. He explains that the message of the cross may seem foolish to the world, but it is the power and wisdom of God. Believers find their wisdom in Christ's crucifixion and redemption.

3. Boasting in the Lord (1 Corinthians 1:26-31): Paul underscores that God has chosen the weak and foolish things of the world to shame the wise and strong. He encourages the Corinthians to boast in the Lord, not in human wisdom or abilities. The ultimate source of wisdom, righteousness, sanctification, and redemption is found in Christ.

The central theme in 1 Corinthians chapter 1 is the call for unity among believers and the contrast between human wisdom and the wisdom of God found in Christ, particularly in the message of the cross. Paul emphasizes the importance of recognizing the centrality of Christ and the gospel message and avoiding divisions and pride based on human wisdom or leaders. This chapter serves as a foundational message on the importance of unity and the ultimate source of wisdom and strength in the Christian faith.

Verse 1:

"Paul, called to be an apostle of Jesus Christ through the will of God, and Sosthenes our brother."

In this verse, Paul introduces himself as an apostle, emphasizing his divine calling by God. Sosthenes is mentioned as a fellow believer. Paul's apostleship is not of his own making but is in accordance with God's divine plan.

Verse 2:

"Unto the church of God which is at Corinth, to them that are sanctified in Christ Jesus, called to be saints, with all that in every place call upon the name of Jesus Christ our Lord, both theirs and ours."

Here, Paul addresses the recipients of his letter, the Corinthian church. He describes them as "sanctified in Christ Jesus" and "called to be saints," highlighting their position in Christ as set apart and holy. He also emphasizes the unity of all who call upon the name of Jesus, both in Corinth and elsewhere, reinforcing the universal nature of the Christian faith.

Verse 3:

"Grace be unto you, and peace, from God our Father, and from the Lord Jesus Christ."

Paul offers a customary Christian greeting, wishing the Corinthians grace and peace from both God the Father and the Lord Jesus Christ. This highlights the importance of the Father and the Son in the Christian faith.

Verse 4:

"I thank my God always on your behalf, for the grace of God which is given you by Jesus Christ."

Paul expresses gratitude for the Corinthians, recognizing the grace of God given to them through Jesus Christ. This emphasizes the role of God's grace in the lives of believers.

Verse 5:

"That in everything ye are enriched by him, in all utterance, and in all knowledge."

Paul acknowledges the Corinthians' enrichment in spiritual gifts, including the ability to speak and understand spiritual truths. These gifts are attributed to Christ's work in their lives.

Verse 6:

"Even as the testimony of Christ was confirmed in you."

The Corinthians' spiritual enrichment serves as confirmation of their relationship with Christ, and their testimony of Him.

Verse 7:

"So that ye come behind in no gift, waiting for the coming of our Lord Jesus Christ."

Paul reassures them that they lack no spiritual gift, and he encourages them to eagerly anticipate the return of Jesus Christ. This serves as a reminder of the future hope in Christ.

Verse 8:

"Who shall also confirm you unto the end, that ye may be blameless in the day of our Lord Jesus Christ."

Paul assures the Corinthians that God will sustain them until the end, ensuring their blamelessness on the day of Christ's return. This emphasizes the believer's security in Christ.

Verse 9:

"God is faithful, by whom ye were called unto the fellowship of his Son Jesus Christ our Lord."

This verse underscores the faithfulness of God, who called the Corinthians into a relationship of fellowship with His Son, Jesus Christ. It highlights the relational aspect of Christianity.

Verse 10:

"Now I beseech you, brethren, by the name of our Lord Jesus Christ, that ye all speak the same thing, and that there be no divisions among you; but that ye be perfectly joined together in the same mind and in the same judgment."

Paul begins to address a major issue in the Corinthian church – division. He implores them to be united in their beliefs and to avoid divisions, emphasizing the importance of unity and like-mindedness among believers.

This commentary provides insight into the opening verses of 1 Corinthians, focusing on Paul's introduction, the grace of God, the enrichment of the Corinthians, and the call to unity in the church.

Verse 11:

"For it hath been declared unto me of you, my brethren, by them which are of the house of Chloe, that there are contentions among you."

In this verse, Paul mentions that he has received reports from Chloe's household about divisions and contentions within the Corinthian church. This is the beginning of his address to the issue of division in the church.

Verse 12:

"Now this I say, that every one of you saith, I am of Paul, and I of Apollos, and I of Cephas, and I of Christ."

Paul highlights the specific cause of the division: the Corinthians aligning themselves with different leaders or teachers, such as himself (Paul), Apollos, Cephas (Peter), and even Christ. This divisive behavior is a source of concern.

Verse 13:

"Is Christ divided? was Paul crucified for you? or were ye baptized in the name of Paul?"

Paul questions the Corinthians, challenging them with the idea that Christ cannot be divided. He reminds them that he was not crucified for them, and they were not baptized in his name. This emphasizes that their primary allegiance should be to Christ, not to human leaders.

Verse 14:

"I thank God that I baptized none of you, but Crispus and Gaius."

Paul expresses gratitude that he did not personally baptize many of the Corinthians, except for Crispus and Gaius. He does this to distance himself from any perception of creating a faction around his own baptism.

Verse 15:

"Lest any should say that I had baptized in mine own name."

Paul is concerned that if he had baptized more Corinthians, it might have led to the misconception that he was forming a following around himself. By baptizing only a few, he avoids such an issue and keeps the focus on Christ.

These verses provide insight into the specific problem of division in the Corinthian church, stemming from allegiances to different leaders and teachers. Paul emphasizes the importance of unity in Christ and not in human leaders. He also takes steps to prevent any misunderstanding that he is seeking to promote himself through baptism.

Verse 16:

"And I baptized also the household of Stephanas: besides, I know not whether I baptized any other."

In this verse, Paul mentions that he baptized the household of Stephanas, but he is uncertain whether he baptized anyone else in Corinth. He continues to emphasize that his role in baptism was minimal, preventing the Corinthians from overly associating with him as a leader.

Verse 17:

"For Christ sent me not to baptize, but to preach the gospel: not with wisdom of words, lest the cross of Christ should be made of none effect."

Paul clarifies his primary mission, which is not focused on baptizing but on preaching the gospel. He emphasizes that his approach to preaching is not characterized by eloquent and persuasive words but by a simple message centered on the cross of Christ. The efficacy of the message is more important than the eloquence of the messenger.

Verse 18:

"For the preaching of the cross is to them that perish foolishness, but unto us which are saved it is the power of God."

Paul contrasts the response to the message of the cross. To those who are perishing in unbelief, it may seem foolish, but to believers, it is the powerful work of God. This underscores the transformative impact of the gospel on those who accept it.

Verse 19:

"For it is written, I will destroy the wisdom of the wise, and will bring to nothing the understanding of the prudent."

Paul quotes the Old Testament (Isaiah 29:14) to support his point. God's wisdom often confounds the wisdom of the world, and He has a way of nullifying the understanding of the worldly-wise.

Verse 20:

"Where is the wise? where is the scribe? where is the disputer of this world? hath not God made foolish the wisdom of this world?"

Paul continues to challenge the wisdom of the world, asking where the worldly wise, scribes, and debaters are. He asserts that God has rendered the wisdom of this world foolish in comparison to divine wisdom.

Verse 21:

"For after that in the wisdom of God the world by wisdom knew not God, it pleased God by the foolishness of preaching to save them that believe."

Paul contrasts the world's inability to know God through human wisdom with God's choice to use the "foolishness of preaching" to save those who believe. This underscores God's sovereignty and the transformative power of the gospel.

Verse 22:

"For the Jews require a sign, and the Greeks seek after wisdom."

Paul acknowledges the differing expectations of the Jews and the Greeks. The Jews look for signs and miracles as evidence, while the Greeks value worldly wisdom. However, the message of the cross transcends these expectations, as it offers a different kind of wisdom and a sign of God's redemptive plan.

These verses highlight the contrast between divine wisdom and the wisdom of the world, with an emphasis on the power of the message of the cross. Paul's mission is to preach the gospel, and he affirms that this message may appear foolish to some but is the power of God unto salvation for those who believe.

Verse 23:

"But we preach Christ crucified, unto the Jews a stumbling block, and unto the Greeks foolishness."

Paul presents the core of his message: the preaching of Christ crucified. This message is a stumbling block to the Jews, as it did not align with their expectations of a powerful Messiah, and it appears foolish to the Greeks, who were accustomed to sophisticated philosophy. The cross, representing suffering and apparent weakness, challenges conventional thinking.

Verse 24:

"But unto them which are called, both Jews and Greeks, Christ the power of God, and the wisdom of God."

For those who are called and have faith, both Jews and Greeks, the message of Christ crucified is not a stumbling block or foolishness. Instead, they recognize it as the power and wisdom of God. This verse underscores the transformative nature of the gospel for those who believe.

Verse 25:

"Because the foolishness of God is wiser than men, and the weakness of God is stronger than men."

Paul asserts that even what might appear as "foolishness" or "weakness" in God's plan is, in reality, wiser and stronger than human wisdom and strength. This emphasizes the divine wisdom and power behind the message of the cross.

Verse 26:

"For ye see your calling, brethren, how that not many wise men after the flesh, not many mighty, not many noble, are called."

Paul reminds the Corinthians that when they reflect on their own calling to faith, they will realize that not many of them were considered wise, mighty, or noble in the worldly sense. This reinforces the idea that God's choice does not align with worldly standards.

Verse 27:

"But God hath chosen the foolish things of the world to confound the wise, and God hath chosen the weak things of the world to confound the things which are mighty."

God's choice is intentional. He selects those considered foolish and weak by the world's standards to confound and humble the worldly-wise and powerful. This is a reflection of God's divine wisdom and sovereignty.

Verse 28:

"And base things of the world, and things which are despised, hath God chosen, yea, and things which are not, to bring to nought things that are."

Paul extends this idea further, emphasizing that God chooses base and despised things and even things that don't exist in human estimation to nullify the things that the world values. This illustrates God's ability to work through the unexpected and humble the proud.
Verse 29:

"That no flesh should glory in his presence."

Ultimately, the purpose of God's unconventional choices is to prevent anyone from boasting or glorying in their own achievements or wisdom in His presence. It redirects all glory to God, acknowledging His role in salvation.
Verse 30:

"But of him are ye in Christ Jesus, who of God is made unto us wisdom, and righteousness, and sanctification, and redemption."

Paul emphasizes that our connection to Christ is not of our own doing but is from God. In Christ, we find wisdom, righteousness, sanctification (holiness), and redemption. All of these blessings come from God and are available to believers through Christ.
Verse 31:

"That, according as it is written, He that glorieth, let him glory in the Lord."

Paul concludes by quoting the Old Testament (Jeremiah 9:23-24) to emphasize that if anyone is to boast, it should be in the Lord, not in their own accomplishments or wisdom. This echoes the central theme of giving all glory to God.

These verses in 1 Corinthians 1:22-32 highlight the contrast between human wisdom and God's wisdom, emphasizing the transformative power of the message of the cross. God's choice of the foolish, weak, and despised demonstrates His wisdom and sovereignty, redirecting all glory to Him. Believers find their wisdom, righteousness, sanctification, and redemption in Christ, and any boasting should be in the Lord.

CHAPTER 2
Wisdom and Knowledge

1 Corinthians Chapter 2 is addressed to the same audience as the rest of the First Corinthians letter. It is written to the "church of God which is at Corinth" (1 Corinthians 1:2), which refers to the Christian community in the city of Corinth. The Apostle Paul's letter to the Corinthians is directed at the members of this church, and in chapter 2, he continues to provide guidance, instruction, and spiritual insight to the Corinthian Christians regarding various matters relevant to their faith and Christian walk.

1 Corinthians Chapter 2 primarily focuses on the theme of wisdom and knowledge in the context of the Christian faith. The chapter can be summarized as follows:

1. The Message of the Cross (1 Corinthians 2:1-5): Paul begins by explaining his approach when he first came to Corinth. He didn't rely on eloquent speech or human wisdom but preached the message of the cross with a demonstration of the Spirit's power. This is to show that faith should not rest on human wisdom but on the power of God.

2. God's Wisdom Revealed (1 Corinthians 2:6-10): Paul discusses the wisdom of God, which is hidden from the rulers of this age but revealed to those who are mature in their faith. This wisdom was a mystery, hidden in the past, but has now been made known through the Spirit. It involves the deep things of God.

3. The Role of the Spirit (1 Corinthians 2:11-16): Paul explains that the wisdom of God is discerned spiritually and not through human understanding alone. Those who have the Spirit of God can understand and judge all things, including the deep things of God. He contrasts the natural person (without the Spirit) and the spiritual person (with the Spirit).

4. Spiritual Wisdom and the Mind of Christ (1 Corinthians 2:16): The chapter ends with a reference to having "the mind of Christ," which is a spiritual wisdom and understanding that comes from the Holy Spirit.

In summary, 1 Corinthians 2 emphasizes that the wisdom of God, particularly as revealed in the message of the cross, transcends human wisdom and understanding. It underscores the role of the Holy Spirit in imparting spiritual wisdom to believers, enabling them to discern and grasp the deep truths of God. The chapter emphasizes the contrast between worldly wisdom and the wisdom that comes from God through the Spirit.

Verse 1:

"And I, brethren, when I came to you, came not with excellency of speech or of wisdom, declaring unto you the testimony of God."

Paul begins this passage by reminding the Corinthians that when he initially arrived to preach to them, he did not rely on eloquent speech or worldly wisdom. Instead, his focus was solely on conveying the testimony of God.

Verse 2:

"For I determined not to know anything among you, save Jesus Christ, and him crucified."

Paul's primary focus in his preaching was Jesus Christ and His crucifixion. He chose to preach a simple message, emphasizing the significance of Christ's death on the cross as the central theme of his ministry.

Verse 3:

"And I was with you in weakness, and in fear, and in much trembling."

Paul acknowledges his own human weaknesses and emotions during his time with the Corinthians. This highlights his reliance on God's power rather than his personal strength.

Verse 4:

"And my speech and my preaching was not with enticing words of man's wisdom, but in demonstration of the Spirit and of power."

Paul reiterates that his preaching was not characterized by persuasive and clever human rhetoric. Instead, it was accompanied by a demonstration of the Spirit's power, underscoring the divine authority behind his message.

Verse 5:

"That your faith should not stand in the wisdom of men, but in the power of God."

Paul's purpose in this approach was to ensure that the Corinthians' faith was not rooted in human wisdom or persuasive words, but in the power of God. He wanted their belief to be based on a foundation of divine power.

Verse 6:

"Howbeit we speak wisdom among them that are perfect: yet not the wisdom of this world, nor of the princes of this world, that come to nought."

Paul acknowledges that there is a form of wisdom that he imparts to mature believers. However, this wisdom is not worldly wisdom or the wisdom of worldly rulers, which ultimately comes to nothing.

Verse 7:

"But we speak the wisdom of God in a mystery, even the hidden wisdom, which God ordained before the world unto our glory."

The wisdom Paul speaks of is the wisdom of God, often veiled in mystery. This hidden wisdom, ordained by God before the world began, is intended for the glory and benefit of believers.

Verse 8:

"Which none of the princes of this world knew: for had they known it, they would not have crucified the Lord of glory."

This hidden wisdom of God was not understood by the worldly rulers of the time. Had they comprehended it, they would not have crucified Jesus, who is described as the "Lord of glory." This reflects the profound nature of God's divine plan.

Verse 9:

"But as it is written, Eye hath not seen, nor ear heard, neither have entered into the heart of man, the things which God hath prepared for them that love him."

Paul quotes the Old Testament (Isaiah 64:4) to emphasize the profound nature of God's plan. Human senses and understanding cannot grasp the full extent of the blessings and revelations God has prepared for those who love Him.

Verse 10:

"But God hath revealed them unto us by his Spirit: for the Spirit searcheth all things, yea, the deep things of God."

Paul concludes by explaining that these hidden mysteries have been revealed to believers through the Holy Spirit. The Spirit of God searches the deep things of God and imparts knowledge and understanding to those who are in a relationship with Him.

In 1 Corinthians 2:1-10, Paul emphasizes the simplicity of his preaching, focusing on the message of Christ crucified and relying on the power of the Spirit. He distinguishes between worldly wisdom and the hidden wisdom of God, which is revealed to believers through the Holy Spirit. The passage highlights the profound nature of God's plan and the role of the Spirit in imparting divine wisdom.

Verse 11:

"For what man knoweth the things of a man, save the spirit of man which is in him? even so the things of God knoweth no man, but the Spirit of God."

Paul begins by drawing a parallel between human knowledge and divine knowledge. He asserts that just as a person's inner thoughts and feelings are known only to themselves, the thoughts and wisdom of God are known only to the Spirit of God. This verse underscores the necessity of the Holy Spirit in understanding and discerning God's wisdom.

Verse 12:

"Now we have received, not the spirit of the world, but the spirit which is of God; that we might know the things that are freely given to us of God."

Paul highlights that believers have received the Spirit of God, not the spirit of the world. This divine Spirit enables them to understand and appreciate the gifts that God has freely bestowed upon them. These gifts include spiritual wisdom and knowledge.

Verse 13:

"Which things also we speak, not in the words which man's wisdom teacheth, but which the Holy Ghost teacheth; comparing spiritual things with spiritual."

Paul emphasizes that when speaking about spiritual matters, he does not rely on human wisdom but rather on the guidance of the Holy Spirit. The Holy Spirit teaches spiritual truths, and Paul conveys these truths using spiritual language, making comparisons between spiritual concepts.

Verse 14:

"But the natural man receiveth not the things of the Spirit of God: for they are foolishness unto him; neither can he know them, because they are spiritually discerned."

Paul introduces the idea of the "natural man" – someone who does not have the indwelling Spirit of God. Such a person cannot comprehend the things of the Spirit because they appear foolish to them. Spiritual truths can only be understood through spiritual discernment, which comes from the Holy Spirit.

Verse 15:

"But he that is spiritual judgeth all things, yet he himself is judged of no man."

Paul contrasts the spiritual person with the natural person. The spiritual person can make sound judgments about all matters, guided by the Spirit. However, they themselves are not subject to the judgments of those who lack spiritual understanding.

Verse 16:

"For who hath known the mind of the Lord, that he may instruct him? But we have the mind of Christ."

Paul quotes from the Old Testament (Isaiah 40:13) to emphasize the unknowable nature of God's mind and His perfect wisdom. However, Paul reassures believers that they have the mind of Christ, which is made accessible to them through the Holy Spirit. This enables them to understand and align with God's will.

Verse 17:

"And I, brethren, could not speak unto you as unto spiritual, but as unto carnal, even as unto babes in Christ."

Paul expresses his disappointment that he could not address the Corinthians as spiritual mature believers but had to speak to them as if they were still spiritually immature, or "babes in Christ." He had to use simpler language and concepts due to their lack of spiritual growth.

Verse 18:

"I have fed you with milk, and not with meat: for hitherto ye were not able to bear it, neither yet now are ye able."

Paul likens his teaching to feeding them with spiritual "milk" rather than "meat." This means that he has provided them with basic, elementary teachings because they were not yet capable of comprehending deeper spiritual truths. Even at this point, he suggests that they are still not ready for more advanced instruction.

Verse 19:

"For ye are yet carnal: for whereas there is among you envying, and strife, and divisions, are ye not carnal, and walk as men?"

Paul rebukes the Corinthians for their continued carnality, which is evident in the presence of envy, strife, and divisions among them. He questions whether they are truly living according to the Spirit or merely behaving like ordinary, worldly people.

Verse 20:

"For while one saith, I am of Paul; and another, I am of Apollos; are ye not carnal?"

Paul points out the factionalism among the Corinthians, where they identify themselves with various leaders, such as Paul and Apollos. This division and attachment to human leaders reflects their carnal and immature state.

In 1 Corinthians 2:11-20, Paul emphasizes the role of the Holy Spirit in understanding spiritual wisdom and knowledge. He distinguishes between the natural person and the spiritual person, highlighting the limitations of human wisdom in comprehending spiritual truths. He underscores the need for spiritual discernment and concludes by addressing the Corinthians' spiritual immaturity, marked by divisions and factionalism.

Carnal Behavior and Spiritual Maturity in the Church

The theme of 1 Corinthians chapter 3 is "Carnal Behavior and Spiritual Maturity in the Church." In this chapter, the Apostle Paul addresses the issue of division and immaturity within the Corinthian church, emphasizing the need for spiritual growth and unity among the believers. Here is an overview of the main themes and points in 1 Corinthians chapter 3:

1. Division and Immaturity (1 Corinthians 3:1-4): Paul begins by chastising the Corinthians for their divisive and immature behavior. He refers to them as "carnal" or "worldly" because they are still acting in a fleshly, divisive manner, characterized by jealousy and strife. They are not demonstrating the maturity that should come with their faith in Christ.

2. The Role of Church Leaders (1 Corinthians 3:5-9): Paul emphasizes that church leaders, including himself and Apollos, are merely servants of God. Their role is to plant and water, but it is God who gives the growth. He underscores the importance of working together as fellow laborers for the common goal.

3. The Foundation of the Church (1 Corinthians 3:10-15): Paul uses the metaphor of a building to describe the church. He asserts that Jesus Christ is the foundation, and believers should take care how they build on it. The quality of each person's work will be tested by fire, and only what is built on the foundation of Christ will endure.

4. The Temple of God (1 Corinthians 3:16-17): Paul reminds the Corinthians that collectively, they are the temple of God, and the Spirit of God dwells in them. He warns against defiling the temple, which likely includes divisions and other sinful behaviors.

5. Worldly Wisdom vs. God's Wisdom (1 Corinthians 3:18-23): Paul contrasts worldly wisdom with the wisdom of God. He encourages the Corinthians not to boast in human wisdom and power but to recognize that all things, including their leaders, belong to them as believers, and they belong to Christ.

The central theme in 1 Corinthians chapter 3 is the need for spiritual maturity, unity, and a focus on Christ as the foundation of the church. Paul rebukes divisions and challenges the Corinthians to grow in their understanding and behavior, recognizing that they are God's temple and should build on the foundation of Christ with care and diligence.

Verse 1:

"And I, brethren, could not speak unto you as unto spiritual, but as unto carnal, even as unto babes in Christ."

Paul begins this chapter by addressing the Corinthians and expressing his frustration. He laments that he cannot address them as spiritually mature believers but must speak to them as if they are still worldly and immature, like "babes in Christ." Despite the time that has passed since their conversion, they have not made the spiritual progress expected of them.

Verse 2:

"I have fed you with milk, and not with meat: for hitherto ye were not able to bear it, neither yet now are ye able."

Paul likens his teaching to feeding them with spiritual "milk" rather than "meat." This means that he has provided them with basic, elementary teachings because they were not yet capable of comprehending deeper spiritual truths. Even at this point, he suggests that they are still not ready for more advanced instruction.

Verse 3:

"For ye are yet carnal: for whereas there is among you envying, and strife, and divisions, are ye not carnal, and walk as men?"

Paul rebukes the Corinthians for their continued carnality, which is evident in the presence of envy, strife, and divisions among them. He questions whether they are truly living according to the Spirit or merely behaving like ordinary, worldly people. These divisions and quarrels indicate their immaturity and inability to live in accordance with the teachings of Christ.

Verse 4:

"For while one saith, I am of Paul; and another, I am of Apollos; are ye not carnal?"

Paul points out the factionalism among the Corinthians, where they identify themselves with various leaders, such as Paul and Apollos. This division and attachment to human leaders reflects their carnal and immature state. Such allegiances to human leaders should not overshadow their allegiance to Christ.

Verse 5:

"Who then is Paul, and who is Apollos, but ministers by whom ye believed, even as the Lord gave to every man?"

Paul reminds the Corinthians that he and Apollos are simply ministers or servants of God through whom they came to faith. It was the Lord who enabled their ministry and called the Corinthians to belief. This reaffirms that leaders in the church should not be the focus; instead, it is the Lord who deserves the primary allegiance.

Verse 6:

"I have planted, Apollos watered, but God gave the increase."

Paul uses the metaphor of planting and watering to describe their roles in the Corinthians' spiritual growth. He planted the initial seeds of faith, and Apollos continued the work. However, the ultimate growth and increase in faith come from God. This reinforces that it is God who brings about spiritual growth, and human leaders play a secondary role.

Verse 7:

"So then neither is he that planteth anything, neither he that watereth, but God that giveth the increase."

Paul makes it clear that neither the one who plants (himself) nor the one who waters (Apollos) hold any significance in comparison to God, who is the one responsible for the spiritual growth. This underscores the idea that all glory and credit should be attributed to God, not to human leaders.

Verse 8:

"Now he that planteth and he that watereth are one: and every man shall receive his own reward according to his own labor."

Paul emphasizes that both the one who plants and the one who waters are working together for the same purpose and are ultimately one in their service to God. However, each person's labor will be rewarded based on their own efforts and faithfulness to the task.

Verse 9:

"For we are laborers together with God: ye are God's husbandry, ye are God's building."

Paul characterizes himself and Apollos as fellow workers with God. He also describes the Corinthians as God's field (husbandry) and God's building, highlighting that their spiritual growth and development are in God's hands.

Verse 10:

"According to the grace of God which is given unto me, as a wise master builder, I have laid the foundation, and another buildeth thereon. But let every man take heed how he buildeth thereupon."

Paul acknowledges that he was granted the grace of God to function as a wise master builder who laid the foundation for the Corinthian church. He then reminds all believers that they have a role in building upon that foundation, and they should be cautious about how they contribute to the spiritual growth of the church. This verse emphasizes the responsibility of all believers to build upon the foundation of faith wisely.

In 1 Corinthians 3:1-10, Paul addresses the immaturity and division among the Corinthians. He laments their carnality and inability to receive deeper spiritual teachings. He rebukes the factionalism in the church, underlining the need for unity and the ultimate role of God in spiritual growth. He also highlights that everyone has a role in building upon the foundation of faith laid by God's grace, and this should be done with care and wisdom.

Verse 11:

"For other foundation can no man lay than that is laid, which is Jesus Christ."

Paul asserts the absolute centrality of Jesus Christ as the foundation of the Christian faith. No other foundation can be laid, and all Christian beliefs and practices are built upon this unshakable foundation. Christ is the cornerstone of the church.

Verse 12:

"Now if any man builds upon this foundation gold, silver, precious stones, wood, hay, stubble;"

Paul uses metaphors to describe the different ways in which individuals may contribute to the growth of the church. "Gold, silver, and precious stones" represent valuable, enduring, and spiritually significant contributions. "Wood, hay, and stubble" represent less valuable or temporary contributions.

Verse 13:

"Every man's work shall be made manifest: for the day shall declare it, because it shall be revealed by fire; and the fire shall try every man's work of what sort it is."

Paul explains that everyone's contributions will ultimately be revealed and evaluated. The metaphorical fire represents a purifying and testing process, revealing the quality of each person's work. The Day of Judgment will make evident the true value of their contributions.

Verse 14:

"If any man's work abides which he hath built thereupon, he shall receive a reward."

For those whose contributions withstand the testing process, they will receive a reward from God. This reward is not specified, but it

implies a recognition of their faithful service and dedication to building upon the foundation of Christ.
Verse 15:

"If any man's work shall be burned, he shall suffer loss: but he himself shall be saved; yet so as by fire."

On the other hand, if a person's contributions do not stand the test and are consumed by the metaphorical fire, they will suffer a loss of potential rewards. However, the person's salvation is secure, though it may be as though they barely escape the fire.
Verse 16:

"Know ye not that ye are the temple of God, and that the Spirit of God dwelleth in you?"

Paul reminds the Corinthians that collectively, as the church, they are the temple of God. The presence of the Holy Spirit dwells within them, emphasizing the sanctity and significance of the church as the dwelling place of God.
Verse 17:

"If any man defiles the temple of God, him shall God destroy; for the temple of God is holy, which temple ye are."

Paul warns against those who would defile the temple of God, which is the church. Such individuals will face judgment from God. The church is holy and must be treated with reverence and respect.
Verse 18:

"Let no man deceive himself. If any man among you seemeth to be wise in this world, let him become a fool, that he may be wise."

Paul advises against self-deception and urges humility. Those who appear wise in the worldly sense should be willing to become "fools" in their own estimation, recognizing their dependence on God's wisdom. True wisdom comes from God, not worldly acclaim.
Verse 19:

"For the wisdom of this world is foolishness with God. For it is written, He taketh the wise in their own craftiness."

Paul reinforces the contrast between worldly wisdom and God's wisdom. Human wisdom is foolishness in God's eyes. He quotes the Old Testament (Job 5:13) to emphasize that the worldly-wise can be ensnared by their own cunning.

Verse 20:

"And again, The Lord knoweth the thoughts of the wise, that they are vain."

Paul quotes another Old Testament passage (Psalm 94:11) to remind the Corinthians that God discerns the futility of human wisdom. The thoughts of the wise, when detached from God's wisdom, are ultimately in vain.

Verse 21:

"Therefore, let no man glory in men. For all things are yours;"

Paul reiterates the message to not boast in human leaders or wisdom. He reminds the Corinthians that, as believers, they possess everything they need in Christ. All things are at their disposal, as they are God's heirs and beneficiaries.

Verse 22:

"Whether Paul, or Apollos, or Cephas, or the world, or life, or death, or things present, or things to come; all are yours;"

Paul expands on the idea of all things being theirs. Whether it's various Christian leaders (Paul, Apollos, Cephas), the world, life, death, present circumstances, or future events, all belong to the Corinthians as beneficiaries of God's grace.

Verse 23:

"And ye are Christ's; and Christ is God's."

Paul concludes by affirming the Corinthians' identity as belonging to Christ, who, in turn, belongs to God. This hierarchy reflects the divine order and emphasizes the interconnectedness of believers with Christ and God.

In 1 Corinthians 3:11-23, Paul emphasizes the absolute centrality of Jesus Christ as the foundation of the Christian faith. He employs metaphors to describe how individuals contribute to the growth of the church and the testing process of their contributions. Paul reminds the Corinthians of the sanctity of the church as God's temple and warns against defiling it. He contrasts worldly wisdom with God's wisdom and encourages humility. He affirms that believers possess everything in Christ and belong to Christ, who belongs to God.

CHAPTER 4

Servants of Christ and Stewards of God's Mysteries

The theme of 1 Corinthians chapter 4 is "Servants of Christ and Stewards of God's Mysteries." In this chapter, the Apostle Paul continues to address the issues within the Corinthian church, focusing on the role of Christian leaders, particularly himself and Apollos, as servants of Christ and stewards of God's mysteries. Here's an overview of the main themes and points in 1 Corinthians chapter 4:

1. Accountability of Servants (1 Corinthians 4:1-2): Paul begins by describing the role of Christian leaders as servants and stewards of the mysteries of God. He emphasizes the requirement of faithfulness and trustworthiness in this role.

2. Humility and Judgment (1 Corinthians 4:3-5): Paul discusses the danger of passing judgment on leaders, emphasizing that it is the

Lord who ultimately judges. He encourages humility among believers and reminds them not to judge prematurely.

3. Irony and Sarcasm (1 Corinthians 4:6-13): Paul employs irony and sarcasm in addressing the Corinthians. He highlights their self-importance and contrasts it with the hardships he and other apostles endure for the sake of the Gospel.

4. Fatherly Exhortation (1 Corinthians 4:14-21): Paul addresses the Corinthians as his beloved children in the faith. He urges them to imitate him as a spiritual father and follow his example. He plans to visit them and offers the choice of discipline or a loving visit.

The central theme in 1 Corinthians chapter 4 revolves around the proper understanding of Christian leadership and the need for humility, trustworthiness, and a focus on God's judgment rather than human judgment. Paul seeks to correct the Corinthians' attitudes and behavior concerning their leaders and reminds them of the sacrifices and hardships endured by those who serve as stewards of God's mysteries.

Verse 1:

"Let a man so account of us, as of the ministers of Christ, and stewards of the mysteries of God."

Paul begins by urging the Corinthians to view him and other Christian leaders not as celebrities or lords but as "ministers of Christ" and "stewards of the mysteries of God." This underscores the responsibility and accountability that leaders have in managing and teaching God's truth.

Verse 2:

"Moreover, it is required in stewards, that a man be found faithful."

Paul emphasizes the primary requirement for stewards, which is faithfulness. Leaders are entrusted with God's truths, and their primary responsibility is to be faithful and trustworthy in handling these truths.

Verse 3:

"But with me it is a very small thing that I should be judged of you, or of man's judgment: yea, I judge not mine own self."

Paul expresses his perspective on human judgment. He does not consider it significant to be judged by the Corinthians or any human court of opinion. He even refrains from passing judgment on himself, as he ultimately leaves judgment to God.

Verse 4:

"For I know nothing by myself; yet am I not hereby justified: but he that judgeth me is the Lord."

Paul clarifies that even though he is not conscious of any wrongdoing, this doesn't automatically justify him. He acknowledges that it is the Lord who ultimately judges him, and His judgment is the final word.

Verse 5:

"Therefore, judge nothing before the time, until the Lord come, who both will bring to light the hidden things of darkness, and will make manifest the counsels of the hearts: and then shall every man have praise of God."

Paul advises against hasty and premature judgment of others. He highlights that the final judgment belongs to the Lord and will occur at His coming. At that time, hidden things, secret intentions, and motives of hearts will be revealed, and God will bestow praise or reward based on His righteous judgment.

Verse 6:

"And these things, brethren, I have in a figure transferred to myself and to Apollos for your sakes; that ye might learn in us not to think of men above that which is written, that no one of you be puffed up for one against another."

Paul uses himself and Apollos as examples for the Corinthians to learn from. He wants to teach them not to exalt human leaders beyond what is written in God's Word. This helps prevent arrogance, division, and unhealthy rivalry among believers.

Verse 7:

"For who maketh thee to differ from another? and what hast thou that thou didst not receive? now if thou didst receive it, why dost thou glory, as if thou hadst not received it?"

Paul challenges the Corinthians to reflect on their differences and unique spiritual gifts. He emphasizes that everything they have, including their spiritual gifts, is ultimately received from God. Therefore, there is no room for boasting as if they had not received these blessings from God.

Verse 8:

"Now ye are full, now ye are rich, ye have reigned as kings without us: and I would to God ye did reign, that we also might reign with you."

Paul employs irony, expressing that the Corinthians see themselves as spiritually "full" and "rich," even believing they are reigning as kings. He wishes they truly were reigning, as it would mean they are living in the fullness of God's blessings, and Paul and other apostles could share in that joy.

Verse 9:

"For I think that God hath set forth us the apostles last, as it were appointed to death: for we are made a spectacle unto the world, and to angels, and to men."

Paul paints a vivid picture of the apostles as the last in line, as though they were appointed to a life of suffering and martyrdom. They have become a public spectacle, observed by both the world and the spiritual realm, which includes angels.

Verse 10:

"We are fools for Christ's sake, but ye are wise in Christ; we are weak, but ye are strong; ye are honourable, but we are despised."

Paul contrasts the Corinthians' self-perception as "wise" and "strong" in Christ with the apostles' self-identification as "fools" and "weak." The apostles are willing to endure dishonor and hardship for the sake of Christ, in contrast to the Corinthians' self-perceived honor and strength.

In 1 Corinthians 4:1-10, Paul emphasizes the role of Christian leaders as stewards of God's mysteries, requiring faithfulness and making them accountable to the Lord. He warns against hasty judgment, reminds the Corinthians not to exalt human leaders above what is written, and challenges their self-perception of wisdom and strength. Paul also describes the apostles' challenging and often persecuted role in contrast to the Corinthians' self-perceived honor and wisdom.

Verse 11:

"Even unto this present hour we both hunger, and thirst, and are naked, and are buffeted, and have no certain dwellingplace."

Paul describes the hardships he and other apostles endure for the sake of the gospel. They continue to face hunger, thirst, lack of clothing, physical abuse, and instability in terms of a permanent dwelling. This emphasizes their sacrificial commitment to spreading the message of Christ.

Verse 12:

"And labour, working with our own hands: being reviled, we bless; being persecuted, we suffer it:"

Paul further highlights the apostles' diligence in working with their own hands to support themselves. Despite facing revilement and persecution, they respond with blessings and are willing to endure suffering for the sake of their mission.

Verse 13:

"Being defamed, we entreat: we are made as the filth of the world, and are the offscouring of all things unto this day."

Paul acknowledges that the apostles are often falsely accused and defamed. They are treated as the lowest of the low in society, considered the "filth of the world," and subjected to contempt and scorn.

Verse 14:

"I write not these things to shame you, but as my beloved sons I warn you."

Paul clarifies that he is not sharing these hardships to shame the Corinthians but to warn and instruct them. He views them as his beloved children in the faith and wants to convey the reality of apostolic suffering for their benefit.

Verse 15:

"For though ye have ten thousand instructors in Christ, yet have ye not many fathers: for in Christ Jesus, I have begotten you through the gospel."

Paul underscores his unique role as a spiritual father to the Corinthians. While they may have many instructors, Paul takes credit for their spiritual birth through the gospel. He played a pivotal role in their conversion and early Christian growth.

Verse 16:

"Wherefore I beseech you, be ye followers of me."

Paul encourages the Corinthians to imitate him in their Christian walk. This is not an act of pride but an expression of his own imitation of Christ and his desire for the Corinthians to follow the example he sets in serving the Lord.

Verse 17:

"For this cause have I sent unto you Timotheus, who is my beloved son, and faithful in the Lord, who shall bring you into remembrance of my ways which be in Christ, as I teach everywhere in every church."

Paul sends Timothy to the Corinthians, who he refers to as his "beloved son" and a faithful follower of the Lord. Timothy's role is to remind the Corinthians of Paul's teaching and the way of life in Christ, which is consistent with what Paul teaches in all churches.

Verse 18:

"Now some are puffed up, as though I would not come to you."

Paul acknowledges that there are some in the Corinthian church who have become arrogant and "puffed up," possibly thinking that he will not visit them. These individuals may be taking advantage of his absence to assert their own authority.

Verse 19:

"But I will come to you shortly, if the Lord will, and will know, not the speech of them which are puffed up, but the power."

Paul asserts his intention to visit the Corinthians, making it conditional on the Lord's will. When he comes, he is not interested in the eloquence or arrogance of the "puffed up" individuals but in the demonstration of the power of the gospel.

Verse 20:

"For the kingdom of God is not in word, but in power."

Paul emphasizes that the true essence of the kingdom of God does not lie in mere words or eloquence but in the tangible power and transformative effects of the gospel message. This underscores the importance of living out the faith and not just professing it.

Verse 21:

"What will ye? shall I come unto you with a rod, or in love, and in the spirit of meekness?"

Paul presents the Corinthians with a choice. They can decide whether he should visit them with stern discipline ("a rod") or in a spirit of love and gentleness ("meekness"). This choice reflects their behavior and response to his warning and instruction.

In 1 Corinthians 4:11-21, Paul provides a stark contrast between the apostles' hardships and the Corinthians' pride and arrogance. He highlights his role as their spiritual father and encourages them to follow his example. Paul sends Timothy to remind them of his teachings and warns that he will visit them to assess their behavior and their response to his instruction, with the choice of discipline or gentleness left to them. He emphasizes the importance of the kingdom of God being demonstrated in power rather than mere words.

CHAPTER 5

Church Discipline and Holiness

The theme of 1 Corinthians chapter 5 is "Church Discipline and Holiness." In this chapter, the Apostle Paul addresses the issue of immorality within the Corinthian church and provides guidance on how to handle such matters within the Christian community. Here's an overview of the main themes and points in 1 Corinthians chapter 5:

1. Sexual Immorality Rebuked (1 Corinthians 5:1-2): Paul begins by addressing a specific case of sexual immorality within the Corinthian church. He mentions that a man is involved in a sexual relationship with his father's wife, a behavior considered immoral even among non-Christians.

2. The Call for Church Discipline (1 Corinthians 5:3-5): Paul emphasizes the seriousness of the situation and calls for the Corinthians to exercise church discipline by removing the sinful individual from their midst. He speaks of delivering the man to Satan for the destruction of the flesh so that his spirit may be saved in the day of the Lord.

3. The Leaven of Malice (1 Corinthians 5:6-8): Paul uses the metaphor of leaven to illustrate the corrupting influence of sin within the church. He encourages the Corinthians to remove the "old leaven" of malice and wickedness and to celebrate the Christian life with sincerity and truth, symbolized by unleavened bread.

4. Exclusion and Separation (1 Corinthians 5:9-13): Paul clarifies that he is not referring to immoral people outside the church but those who claim to be believers and continue in sin. He instructs the Corinthians not to associate with such individuals and emphasizes that it is the church's responsibility to judge its members.

The central theme in 1 Corinthians chapter 5 is the need for church discipline in response to serious sin within the Christian community. Paul stresses the importance of maintaining holiness and purity within the body of believers and addresses the responsibility of the church to address and correct immoral behavior among its members. This chapter serves as a guide for maintaining moral and spiritual integrity within the local church.

Verse 1:

"It is reported commonly that there is fornication among you, and such fornication as is not so much as named among the Gentiles, that one should have his father's wife."

Paul begins by addressing a specific and serious issue in the Corinthian church. He has received reports that there is a case of sexual immorality, specifically a form of incest, among the members. This offense is so egregious that it is not even mentioned among non-believers (Gentiles), referring to its shocking nature.

Verse 2:

"And ye are puffed up, and have not rather mourned, that he that hath done this deed might be taken away from among you."

Paul rebukes the Corinthians for their pride and arrogance in response to this sin. Instead of being proud, they should have been sorrowful and grieving over the sin committed. He urges them to take appropriate action to remove the offender from their midst.

Verse 3:

"For I verily, as absent in body, but present in spirit, have judged already, as though I were present, concerning him that hath so done this deed,"

Paul asserts his apostolic authority and judgment in this matter, even though he is not physically present in Corinth. He has already passed judgment on the one who committed this sin, as if he were there in person.

Verse 4:

"In the name of our Lord Jesus Christ, when ye are gathered together, and my spirit, with the power of our Lord Jesus Christ,"

Paul invokes the authority of the Lord Jesus Christ. When the Corinthians gather as a church and with Paul's spiritual presence (even in his absence), they should do so in the power and authority of the Lord Jesus Christ.

Verse 5:

"To deliver such a one unto Satan for the destruction of the flesh, that the spirit may be saved in the day of the Lord Jesus."

Paul's instruction is to expel the offender from the church community and deliver them to Satan, which, in this context, likely means excommunicating them. This severe measure is intended to bring about repentance and a change in behavior, ultimately leading to the salvation of the individual's spirit when the Lord Jesus returns.

Verse 6:

"Your glorying is not good. Know ye not that a little leaven leaveneth the whole lump?"

Paul criticizes the Corinthians for their arrogance and misplaced pride. He uses the metaphor of leaven (yeast) to illustrate how a small amount of sin or corruption can influence and permeate the entire community. Their boasting and complacency are dangerous.

Verse 7:

"Purge out therefore the old leaven, that ye may be a new lump, as ye are unleavened. For even Christ our passover is sacrificed for us:"

Paul instructs the Corinthians to cleanse or purge the "old leaven" from their midst. By doing this, they can become a new, pure community. He draws a parallel between the removal of leaven during the Passover feast and the sacrifice of Christ, signifying that Christ's sacrifice has the power to cleanse them of sin.

Verse 8:

"Therefore, let us keep the feast, not with old leaven, neither with the leaven of malice and wickedness; but with the unleavened bread of sincerity and truth."

Paul continues the analogy, encouraging the Corinthians to maintain a holy and sincere lifestyle. They should not engage in malice and wickedness but instead pursue sincerity and truth. In doing so, they are "keeping the feast" in a spiritual sense, maintaining the purity that Christ's sacrifice provides.

Verse 9:

"I wrote unto you in an epistle not to company with fornicators:"

Paul refers to a previous letter he wrote to the Corinthians in which he instructed them not to associate with those engaged in sexual immorality.

Verse 10:

"Yet not altogether with the fornicators of this world, or with the covetous, or extortioners, or with idolaters; for then must ye needs go out of the world."

Paul clarifies that he did not mean to avoid contact with all immoral people in the world because that would be impossible. Believers would have to leave the world entirely. His point is about separation from those within the church who persist in such sins.

Verse 11:

"But now I have written unto you not to keep company, if any man that is called a brother be a fornicator, or covetous, or an idolater, or a railer, or a drunkard, or an extortioner; with such a one no not to eat."

Paul's instruction is clear: if someone in the church claims to be a believer (called a brother) but continues in a pattern of sin, particularly sexual immorality, covetousness, idolatry, slander (railer), drunkenness, or extortion, then other believers should not even eat with that person. This is a form of discipline and separation intended to bring about repentance.

Verse 12:

"For what have I to do to judge them also that are without? do not ye judge them that are within?"

Paul distinguishes between judging those inside the church and those outside. Believers have a responsibility to judge or discipline those within the Christian community, but it is not their role to judge those outside the church; that is God's prerogative.

Verse 13:

"But them that are without God judgeth. Therefore, put away from among yourselves that wicked person."

Paul reaffirms that God will judge those outside the church, while the church should exercise judgment within. As a conclusion, he instructs the Corinthians to remove the wicked person from their midst, following through with the discipline he has prescribed.

In 1 Corinthians 5:1-13, Paul addresses a serious case of sexual immorality within the Corinthian church. He rebukes the Corinthians for their arrogance and instructs them to discipline the offender by expelling him from the community. Paul uses the metaphor of leaven to illustrate the influence of sin and emphasizes the need for purity and sincerity. He clarifies that believers should judge those within the church but not those outside, as God will judge them. The chapter ends with the directive to remove the wicked person from their fellowship.

CHAPTER 6

Settling Disputes and Maintaining Holiness

The theme of 1 Corinthians chapter 6 is "Settling Disputes and Maintaining Holiness." In this chapter, the Apostle Paul addresses the issue of lawsuits among believers, sexual immorality, and the importance of maintaining holiness and purity within the Christian community. Here's an overview of the main themes and points in 1 Corinthians chapter 6:

1. Settling Disputes Among Believers (1 Corinthians 6:1-11): Paul begins by addressing the problem of believers taking legal action against one another in secular courts. He admonishes the Corinthians for not resolving their disputes within the church and suggests that they

should be able to settle such matters among themselves. He reminds them that they will judge the world and even angels, so they should be able to handle these smaller issues.

2. Warning Against Sexual Immorality (1 Corinthians 6:12-20): Paul transitions to the issue of sexual immorality. He warns against sexual sin, emphasizing that believers' bodies are temples of the Holy Spirit and should be kept pure. He argues that sexual immorality is a sin against one's own body and encourages believers to flee from it.

3. Bought with a Price (1 Corinthians 6:19-20): Paul reminds the Corinthians that they have been bought with a price—the blood of Christ. Therefore, they should honor God with their bodies and live in a way that glorifies Him.

The central theme in 1 Corinthians chapter 6 is the need for believers to handle disputes and conflicts within the church, avoiding lawsuits in secular courts. Paul also underscores the importance of sexual purity and maintaining the holiness of one's body, which is indwelt by the Holy Spirit. This chapter serves as a guide for resolving conflicts and maintaining moral and spiritual integrity within the Christian community.

Verse 1:

"Dare any of you, having a matter against another, go to law before the unjust, and not before the saints?"

Paul begins by addressing a situation where members of the Corinthian church are taking their legal disputes before secular or pagan courts rather than seeking resolution within the Christian community. He questions the wisdom of this action.

Verse 2:

"Do ye not know that the saints shall judge the world? and if the world shall be judged by you, are ye unworthy to judge the smallest matters?"

Paul reminds the Corinthians of the future role of believers in judging the world, suggesting that they should have the competence to judge even the smallest disputes within the church. He points out the inconsistency in seeking judgment from unbelievers when they will ultimately judge the world.

Verse 3:

"Know ye not that we shall judge angels? how much more things that pertain to this life?"

Paul adds to the previous point by highlighting the future role of believers in judging angels. He argues that if they will have authority over angels, they should certainly be able to resolve earthly matters or disputes among themselves.

Verse 4:

"If then ye have judgments of things pertaining to this life, set them to judge who are least esteemed in the church."

Paul advises the Corinthians to appoint those who are considered least significant or esteemed within the church to judge matters related to this life. This approach helps maintain order and resolves disputes without the need to involve outsiders.

Verse 5:

"I speak to your shame. Is it so, that there is not a wise man among you? no, not one that shall be able to judge between his brethren?"

Paul expresses disappointment in the Corinthians for not having a wise or discerning person among them who can settle disputes among fellow believers. He expects that there should be someone with the ability to judge and mediate.

Verse 6:

"But brother goeth to law with brother, and that before the unbelievers."

Paul reiterates the issue by highlighting that believers are taking legal action against each other in secular courts, which involves one brother suing another. This not only reflects poorly on the church but also exposes them to the judgment of unbelievers.

Verse 7:

"Now therefore there is utterly a fault among you, because ye go to law one with another. Why do ye not rather take wrong? why do ye not rather suffer yourselves to be defrauded?"

Paul characterizes this behavior as a fault or failure among the Corinthians. He suggests that it would be better for them to endure wrong or accept being defrauded by a fellow believer instead of resorting to legal action against each other. This approach aligns with Christ's teachings on turning the other cheek and loving one's neighbor.

Verse 8:

"Nay, ye do wrong, and defraud, and that your brethren."

Paul makes it clear that not only are the Corinthians wrong in their actions, but they are also committing fraud against their own brothers and sisters in Christ. Their actions are causing harm and division within the Christian community.

Verse 9:

"Know ye not that the unrighteous shall not inherit the kingdom of God? Be not deceived: neither fornicators, nor idolaters, nor adulterers, nor effeminate, nor abusers of themselves with mankind,"

Paul reminds the Corinthians of the consequences of unrighteous behavior. He emphasizes that unrighteous individuals will not inherit the kingdom of God and warns them not to be deceived. He provides a list of specific sins that could exclude individuals from the kingdom of God, including sexual immorality, idolatry, adultery, effeminacy, and homosexuality.

Verse 10:

"Nor thieves, nor covetous, nor drunkards, nor revilers, nor extortioners, shall inherit the kingdom of God."

Paul continues the list of behaviors that can prevent individuals from inheriting the kingdom of God. This includes theft, covetousness, drunkenness, slander (revilers), and extortion. These sins are contrary to the values and principles of God's kingdom.

In 1 Corinthians 6:1-10, Paul addresses the issue of believers taking legal disputes before secular courts rather than resolving them within the church. He argues that believers should be able to judge such matters among themselves and expresses disappointment that they are not able to do so. Paul warns against unrighteous behavior and lists specific sins that can prevent individuals from inheriting the kingdom of God, emphasizing the importance of living in accordance with God's values and principles.

Verse 11:

"And such were some of you: but ye are washed, but ye are sanctified, but ye are justified in the name of the Lord Jesus, and by the Spirit of our God."

Paul reminds the Corinthians of their past lives before coming to faith in Christ. Some of them had been involved in various sins, but through their faith in Jesus Christ, they have been cleansed (washed), set apart for God's holy purpose (sanctified), and declared righteous (justified) in the name of the Lord Jesus and through the power of the Holy Spirit. This verse underscores the transformative power of the gospel in believers' lives.

Verse 12:

"All things are lawful unto me, but all things are not expedient: all things are lawful for me, but I will not be brought under the power of any."

Paul introduces a principle regarding Christian freedom. While believers have freedom in Christ, not everything that is technically permissible is beneficial. Paul refuses to be controlled or dominated by any of these freedoms. This verse highlights the importance of exercising freedom responsibly.

Verse 13:

"Meats for the belly, and the belly for meats: but God shall destroy both it and them. Now the body is not for fornication, but for the Lord; and the Lord for the body."

Paul distinguishes between the purpose of the body and the temporary nature of physical desires. While food is meant for the stomach and vice versa, the body is not meant for sexual immorality. It is intended for serving the Lord, emphasizing that the body is meant for holy purposes and is connected to the Lord.

Verse 14:

"And God hath both raised up the Lord, and will also raise up us by his own power."

Paul reinforces the sanctity of the body by highlighting that God has raised the Lord Jesus from the dead and will also raise believers in the future, demonstrating the body's significance and connection to God's power.

Verse 15:

"Know ye not that your bodies are the members of Christ? shall I then take the members of Christ, and make them the members of a harlot? God forbid."

Paul emphasizes the intimate connection between the believer's body and Christ. He poses a rhetorical question, asking if it's appropriate to take the members of Christ's body and involve them in sexual immorality. His response is a strong "God forbid," indicating that this is entirely inappropriate and contrary to the sanctity of the body as a member of Christ.

Verse 16:

"What? know ye not that he which is joined to a harlot is one body? for two, saith he, shall be one flesh."

Paul references the Old Testament (Genesis 2:24) to illustrate the profound union that occurs through sexual intercourse. When a person is joined to a harlot, they become one body with that person, as the Scripture states, "for two shall be one flesh."

Verse 17:

"But he that is joined unto the Lord is one spirit."

Paul contrasts the union that takes place in sexual relations with the spiritual union believers have with the Lord. Those who are joined to the Lord are one spirit with Him, highlighting the deep spiritual connection between believers and Christ.

Verse 18:

"Flee fornication. Every sin that a man doeth is without the body; but he that committeth fornication sinneth against his own body."

Paul's strong exhortation is to flee from sexual immorality. He distinguishes sexual sin from other sins, emphasizing that it is a sin against one's own body. This underscores the unique seriousness of sexual immorality.

Verse 19:

"What? know ye not that your body is the temple of the Holy Ghost which is in you, which ye have of God, and ye are not your own?"

Paul reiterates the sanctity of the believer's body. The body is described as the temple of the Holy Spirit, a dwelling place for God's presence. Believers are reminded that they do not belong to themselves; they were bought with a price, the blood of Christ, and are now dedicated to serving God.

Verse 20:

"For ye are bought with a price: therefore, glorify God in your body, and in your spirit, which are God's."

Paul concludes with a powerful reminder of the believer's identity and responsibility. Because they have been redeemed by Christ's sacrifice, they are to glorify God in both their bodies and spirits, recognizing that they belong to God. This verse underscores the profound obligation to live in a way that honors and glorifies God in every aspect of their lives.

In 1 Corinthians 6:11-20, Paul emphasizes the transformative power of the gospel, which washes, sanctifies, and justifies believers. He addresses the principle of Christian freedom, urging responsible use of liberties. He underscores the sacredness of the believer's body as a member of Christ and the dwelling place of the Holy Spirit. Sexual immorality is strongly condemned as a sin against one's own body. Believers are reminded of their identity as those bought with a price, tasked with glorifying God in both body and spirit.

CHAPTER 7

Christian Ethics and Relationships

The theme of 1 Corinthians chapter 7 is "Christian Ethics and Relationships." In this chapter, the Apostle Paul addresses various topics related to marriage, singleness, divorce, and Christian living. The central theme revolves around how believers should conduct themselves in different relational situations while upholding Christian principles and ethics. Here's an overview of the main themes and points in 1 Corinthians chapter 7:

1. Marriage and Celibacy (1 Corinthians 7:1-9): Paul begins by discussing the advantages and disadvantages of marriage and singleness.

He advises that each person should remain in the state they were in when they became a believer. He emphasizes that celibacy can provide an opportunity for undivided devotion to the Lord.

2. Marriage to Unbelievers (1 Corinthians 7:10-16): Paul addresses the issue of believers married to unbelievers. He advises believers to remain married to unbelieving spouses as long as the unbelieving spouse is willing to live with them. However, if the unbeliever chooses to leave, the believer is not bound in such cases.

3. Contentment in One's Calling (1 Corinthians 7:17-24): Paul encourages believers to remain in the circumstances in which they were called, whether married or unmarried. He emphasizes that the most important thing is to obey God and serve Him faithfully in one's present state.

4. Advice on Marriage and Betrothals (1 Corinthians 7:25-40): Paul offers practical advice concerning engagements, widows, and virgins. He suggests that people who are not in a committed relationship should consider remaining single to better focus on the Lord's work, but also acknowledges that marriage is a good and honorable choice.

The central theme of 1 Corinthians chapter 7 is how to navigate various relational situations in a manner that aligns with Christian ethics and principles. Paul provides guidance on marriage, celibacy, and interactions with unbelieving spouses, all within the context of living a life devoted to serving and honoring God. This chapter offers practical advice for believers on how to approach relationships in a way that reflects their commitment to Christ.

Verse 1:

"Now concerning the things whereof ye wrote unto me: It is good for a man not to touch a woman."

Paul begins this section by addressing a matter about which the Corinthians had written to him. He initially suggests that it can be good for a man to avoid physical contact with a woman. This may be a response to questions regarding celibacy or self-control within the context of marriage.

Verse 2:

"Nevertheless, to avoid fornication, let every man have his own wife, and let every woman have her own husband."

Paul acknowledges that celibacy and avoiding physical contact can be commendable but recognizes the reality of human nature. To avoid sexual immorality (fornication), he advises that every man should have his own wife, and every woman should have her own husband. This guidance emphasizes the importance of marriage as a legitimate outlet for sexual desires.

Verse 3:

"Let the husband render unto the wife due benevolence: and likewise, also the wife unto the husband."

Paul addresses the mutual responsibilities within marriage. Husbands are to fulfill their conjugal duties to their wives, and wives are to do the same for their husbands. This verse underscores the importance of meeting each other's physical and emotional needs within the marital relationship.

Verse 4:

"The wife hath not power of her own body, but the husband: and likewise, also the husband hath not power of his own body, but the wife."

Paul emphasizes the shared authority and mutual ownership within marriage. Neither the husband nor the wife has exclusive authority over their own bodies; rather, they belong to each other. This concept promotes mutual respect and cooperation within the marriage relationship.

Verse 5:

"Defraud ye not one the other, except it be with consent for a time, that ye may give yourselves to fasting and prayer; and come together again, that Satan tempt you not for your incontinency."

Paul advises against withholding conjugal rights from one another within marriage except by mutual consent for a specific period, dedicated to prayer and fasting. The purpose of this temporary abstinence is to avoid falling into sin due to a lack of self-control (incontinency).

Verse 6:

"But I speak this by permission, and not of commandment."

Paul makes it clear that his advice in this matter is not a commandment from the Lord but rather a concession. He recognizes that this advice allows for personal choice and discretion within the marriage relationship.

Verse 7:

"For I would that all men were even as I myself. But every man hath his proper gift of God, one after this manner, and another after that."

Paul expresses his personal preference for celibacy, which he views as a unique gift from God. He acknowledges that not everyone possesses this gift, and some are naturally inclined toward marriage while others are inclined toward celibacy. He encourages understanding and respecting individual differences.

Verse 8:

"I say, therefore, to the unmarried and widows, it is good for them if they abide even as I."

Paul advises those who are unmarried or widowed that it can be advantageous for them to remain single, following his example of celibacy. However, this is not a command but rather a suggestion for those who have the gift and calling for it.
Verse 9:

"But if they cannot contain, let them marry: for it is better to marry than to burn."

Paul recognizes that not everyone can exercise the self-control required for celibacy. In such cases, he recommends marriage as a better alternative to avoiding the temptation of sexual sin. This verse reflects the practical wisdom of providing an outlet for one's natural desires.
Verse 10:

"And unto the married I command, yet not I, but the Lord, Let not the wife depart from her husband."

In this verse, Paul addresses a different aspect of marriage. He specifies that this is a command not from him but from the Lord Himself. The command is for wives not to depart from their husbands, emphasizing the sanctity of the marriage covenant and the importance of marital commitment.

In 1 Corinthians 7:1-10, Paul provides guidance on marriage, celibacy, and sexual relations within the context of Christian relationships. He acknowledges the value of celibacy but emphasizes the importance of marriage for those who cannot exercise self-control. Paul highlights the mutual responsibilities within marriage and encourages spouses to meet each other's needs. He addresses the concept of abstinence by mutual consent for prayer and fasting. Paul stresses the gift of celibacy and the understanding that not everyone possesses this gift. He also affirms the Lord's command that wives should not depart from their husbands, emphasizing the sanctity of the marriage covenant.

Verse 11:

"But and if she departs, let her remain unmarried, or be reconciled to her husband: and let not the husband put away his wife."

Paul continues addressing marital matters. If a wife chooses to leave her husband, Paul advises her to remain unmarried or seek reconciliation with her husband. He also advises husbands not to divorce their wives. This guidance promotes the importance of preserving marital relationships and seeking reconciliation over separation.

Verse 12:

"But to the rest speak I, not the Lord: If any brother hath a wife that believeth not, and she be pleased to dwell with him, let him not put her away."

Paul distinguishes his own instruction from the Lord's command. He addresses a specific scenario where a believer is married to an unbeliever. In this case, if the unbelieving spouse is willing to live with the believer, Paul advises against divorcing them. This demonstrates the importance of maintaining the marriage, when possible, even when one spouse is a believer and the other is not.

Verse 13:

"And the woman which hath a husband that believeth not, and if he be pleased to dwell with her, let her not leave him."

Paul extends the same advice to believing wives married to unbelieving husbands. If the unbelieving husband is willing to stay in the marriage, the believing wife should not leave him. This emphasizes the importance of preserving the marriage and being a positive influence on the unbelieving spouse.

Verse 14:

"For the unbelieving husband is sanctified by the wife, and the unbelieving wife is sanctified by the husband: else were your children unclean; but now are they holy."

Paul explains that the believing spouse has a sanctifying influence on the unbelieving spouse and their children. This sanctification does not mean that the unbelieving spouse is automatically saved, but it does have a positive influence on the household. This emphasizes the importance of maintaining the marriage and providing a godly environment for the children.
Verse 15:

"But if the unbelieving departs, let him depart. A brother or a sister is not under bondage in such cases: but God hath called us to peace."

If the unbelieving spouse decides to leave the marriage, Paul allows for their departure. In such cases, the believing spouse is not bound or obligated to prevent the departure. The primary concern is maintaining peace in the situation.
Verse 16:

"For what knowest thou, O wife, whether thou shalt save thy husband? or how knowest thou, O man, whether thou shalt save thy wife?"

Paul raises the possibility that the believing spouse's conduct and influence may ultimately lead the unbelieving spouse to faith. This highlights the importance of maintaining the marriage and being a positive Christian witness to one's spouse.
Verse 17:

"But as God hath distributed to every man, as the Lord hath called every one, so let him walk. And so, ordain I in all churches."

Paul emphasizes the importance of living according to the calling and circumstances God has given to each individual. He establishes this as a principle applicable to all churches, urging believers to live out their faith in their specific situations.

Verse 18:

"Is any man called being circumcised? let him not become uncircumcised. Is any called in uncircumcision? let him not be circumcised."

Paul addresses a cultural and religious issue regarding circumcision. He advises believers to remain in the state in which they were called, whether circumcised or uncircumcised. This highlights the idea that one's external religious status is less important than their relationship with God.

Verse 19:

"Circumcision is nothing, and uncircumcision is nothing, but the keeping of the commandments of God."

Paul underscores that the external act of circumcision (or its absence) is not inherently significant. What truly matters is obedience to God's commandments. This reflects a broader principle of spiritual importance over external rituals.

Verse 20:

"Let every man abide in the same calling wherein he was called."

Paul reiterates the idea that believers should continue in the state or calling in which they were when they became Christians. This principle promotes contentment with one's life situation and emphasizes the value of serving God in any circumstance.

In 1 Corinthians 7:11-20, Paul provides guidance on marital relationships, emphasizing the importance of reconciliation and maintaining marriages when possible. He addresses specific scenarios of mixed-belief marriages and encourages believers to remain with unbelieving spouses who are willing to live with them. Paul emphasizes the sanctifying influence of the believing spouse and the importance of preserving a peaceful environment. He also touches on the significance of obedience to God's commandments over external rituals and the value of contentment in one's life situation.

Verse 21:

"Art thou called being a servant? care not for it: but if thou mayest be made free, use it rather."

Paul addresses the situation of a believer who is a servant (slave) when they become a Christian. He advises them not to be overly concerned about their status as a servant. However, if they have the opportunity to gain their freedom, they should take it. This advice reflects the idea that spiritual freedom in Christ is more significant than one's social or legal status.

Verse 22:

"For he that is called in the Lord, being a servant, is the Lord's freeman: likewise, also he that is called, being free, is Christ's servant."

Paul emphasizes the spiritual equality of believers in Christ, regardless of their social status. A servant who becomes a believer is, in the eyes of the Lord, a freeman. Similarly, a free person who comes to Christ becomes His servant. This underlines the transformative power of faith and the universality of the gospel message.

Verse 23:

"Ye are bought with a price; be not ye the servants of men."

Paul reminds believers that they have been redeemed by Christ's sacrifice. Therefore, they should not become slaves to human masters. This message emphasizes the importance of serving Christ and not allowing worldly concerns to enslave them.

Verse 24:

"Brethren, let every man, wherein he is called, therein abide with God."

Paul advises believers to remain in their current circumstances with God. This means that they should serve God faithfully and wholeheartedly regardless of their social or legal status. Contentment and faithfulness in one's current situation are important principles.

Verse 25:

"Now concerning virgins, I have no commandment of the Lord: yet I give my judgment, as one that hath obtained mercy of the Lord to be faithful."

Paul addresses the topic of unmarried individuals, particularly virgins. He clarifies that he is providing his own judgment or advice in this matter, as he has not received a specific commandment from the Lord. His guidance is based on his understanding of God's mercy and his commitment to being faithful.

Verse 26:

"I suppose therefore that this is good for the present distress, I say, that it is good for a man so to be."

Paul offers his opinion that, given the current circumstances or distress, it is good for individuals to remain unmarried. This could be a practical suggestion based on the challenges of the time.

Verse 27:

"Art thou bound unto a wife? seek not to be loosed. Art thou loosed from a wife? seek not a wife."

Paul advises those who are married to remain married and not seek divorce. He also advises those who are not married not to actively seek a marriage partner. This guidance reflects an emphasis on contentment in one's current situation.

Verse 28:

"But and if thou marry, thou hast not sinned; and if a virgin marries, she hath not sinned. Nevertheless, such shall have trouble in the flesh: but I spare you."

Paul clarifies that there is no sin in marrying. However, he acknowledges that marriage can bring its own set of challenges and difficulties. He adds that he is sparing the Corinthians from potential troubles by offering this advice.

Verse 29:

"But this I say, brethren, the time is short: it remaineth, that both they that have wives be as though they had none;"

Paul reminds the believers that the time is short, likely referring to the imminence of Christ's return. He encourages those who are married to live in such a way that their marital status does not overly preoccupy them. They should focus on eternal matters and the kingdom of God.

Verse 30:

"And they that weep, as though they wept not; and they that rejoice, as though they rejoiced not; and they that buy, as though they possessed not;"

Paul extends the idea of living with a sense of the shortness of time to various aspects of life. Believers should not be consumed by sorrow, joy, or material possessions. Instead, they should maintain a perspective that is mindful of eternal priorities and values.

In 1 Corinthians 7:21-30, Paul addresses various aspects of the Christian life, including the status of servants, the spiritual equality of believers, and the importance of not being enslaved to worldly concerns. He offers advice on marriage and celibacy, emphasizing contentment in one's current situation. Paul also reminds believers of the shortness of time and encourages them to prioritize eternal values and the kingdom of God.

Verse 31:

"And they that use this world, as not abusing it: for the fashion of this world passeth away."

Paul reminds the Corinthians that those who engage in the affairs of this world should do so with the awareness that the present world is transitory. Believers should not become overly attached or addicted to the material or temporary aspects of life. Instead, they should prioritize the eternal.

Verse 32:

"But I would have you without carefulness. He that is unmarried careth for the things that belong to the Lord, how he may please the Lord:"

Paul expresses his desire for believers to be free from anxiety or worldly concerns. He observes that unmarried individuals have the capacity to focus their attention on serving the Lord and pleasing Him. This suggests that being unmarried can offer greater freedom to engage in spiritual matters.

Verse 33:

"But he that is married careth for the things that are of the world, how he may please his wife."

Conversely, Paul notes that married individuals have additional responsibilities, particularly in caring for the needs and desires of their spouses. This is a natural part of the marital relationship, and it may lead to divided attention between serving the Lord and pleasing one's spouse.

Verse 34:

"There is a difference also between a wife and a virgin. The unmarried woman careth for the things of the Lord, that she may be holy both in body and in spirit: but she that is married careth for the things of the world, how she may please her husband."

Paul draws a distinction between married women and unmarried virgins. Unmarried women can devote themselves to the things of the Lord, seeking holiness in both body and spirit. In contrast, married women have the responsibility of tending to the concerns of their husbands, which may include worldly matters.

Verse 35:

"And this I speak for your own profit; not that I may cast a snare upon you, but for that which is comely, and that ye may attend upon the Lord without distraction."

Paul reassures the Corinthians that he offers this advice for their benefit. He does not intend to ensnare them but rather to guide them toward what is appropriate and conducive to serving the Lord without being distracted by worldly cares.

Verse 36:

"But if any man thinks that he behaveth himself uncomely toward his virgin, if she passes the flower of her age, and need so require, let him do what he will, he sinneth not: let them marry."

Paul acknowledges that some may find it difficult to control their desires and may believe they are acting improperly toward their unmarried partner. In such cases, he permits them to marry, emphasizing that they are not sinning by doing so. This allows for the moral fulfillment of their desires within marriage.

Verse 37:

"Nevertheless, he that standeth steadfast in his heart, having no necessity, but hath power over his own will, and hath so decreed in his heart that he will keep his virgin, doeth well."

Paul acknowledges that some individuals possess the self-control to remain celibate and have determined to do so. He commends them for their steadfastness and self-discipline. This verse highlights that celibacy is a valid and honorable choice for those who can maintain it.

Verse 38:

"So, then he that giveth her in marriage doeth well, but he that giveth her not in marriage doeth better."

Paul sums up the previous discussion by stating that both marrying and remaining unmarried are good choices. However, he suggests that remaining unmarried may be a better choice if one can maintain that commitment. This reflects his personal opinion on the matter.

Verse 39:

"The wife is bound by the law as long as her husband liveth; but if her husband be dead, she is at liberty to be married to whom she will; only in the Lord."

Paul reiterates the principle that a wife is bound by marriage to her husband as long as he is alive. However, if her husband dies, she is free to marry whomever she chooses, with the condition that the new marriage partner is a believer ("in the Lord").

Verse 40:

"But she is happier if she so abides, after my judgment: and I think also that I have the Spirit of God."

Paul expresses his judgment that a widow may be happier if she remains unmarried, but he acknowledges that his perspective may be influenced by his own judgment and understanding of the Spirit of God. This section concludes Paul's discussion on marriage and celibacy in the context of the Christian life.

CHAPTER 8

Food Offered to Idols and Christian Liberty

The theme of 1 Corinthians chapter 8 is "Food Offered to Idols and Christian Liberty." In this chapter, the Apostle Paul addresses the issue of whether it is acceptable for Christians to eat food that has been sacrificed to idols. The central theme revolves around the balance between Christian liberty and the responsibility not to cause others to stumble in their faith. Here's an overview of the main themes and points in 1 Corinthians chapter 8:

1. Concerns About Food Sacrificed to Idols (1 Corinthians 8:1-3): Paul begins by acknowledging that knowledge puffs up, but love edifies. He addresses the issue of food offered to idols and highlights the balance between knowledge and love in the Christian community.

2. Idols and Their True Nature (1 Corinthians 8:4-6): Paul explains that idols are not real gods, and there is only one true God. He emphasizes that for Christians, there is no other god but the Father, and no other Lord but Jesus Christ.

3. Concern for Weaker Brothers and Sisters (1 Corinthians 8:7-13): Paul addresses the issue of whether it is acceptable to eat food sacrificed to idols. He advises that while Christians have the knowledge that idols are not real, they should consider the conscience of weaker believers who might be stumbled by such actions. He emphasizes the importance of not causing others to sin through one's liberty.

The central theme in 1 Corinthians chapter 8 is the balance between exercising Christian liberty and the responsibility to consider the welfare and conscience of fellow believers. Paul's guidance encourages believers to prioritize love and the well-being of others over their own freedoms, particularly in matters that might lead weaker believers into temptation or confusion regarding their faith.

Verse 1:

"Now as touching things offered unto idols, we know that we all have knowledge. Knowledge puffeth up, but charity edifieth."

Paul introduces the topic of eating food sacrificed to idols, which was a common issue in the Corinthian church. He acknowledges that the Corinthians have knowledge on this matter. However, he emphasizes that knowledge alone can lead to arrogance, but love (charity) builds up the Christian community. In other words, it's not just about knowing what is right or wrong but how that knowledge is applied in love and consideration for others.

Verse 2:

"And if any man thinks that he knoweth anything, he knoweth nothing yet as he ought to know."

Paul cautions against an attitude of overconfidence in one's knowledge. Even those who think they know a lot may not truly understand the implications of their knowledge. True wisdom involves recognizing one's limitations and considering how knowledge affects others.

Verse 3:

"But if any man loves God, the same is known of him."

Paul highlights the central importance of loving God. Those who genuinely love God are known by Him, and this relationship of love should guide their actions and decisions.

Verse 4:

"As concerning, therefore, the eating of those things that are offered in sacrifice unto idols, we know that an idol is nothing in the world, and that there is none other God but one."

Paul begins to address the specific issue of eating food sacrificed to idols. He affirms that idols themselves have no real power or significance in the world. There is only one true God.

Verse 5:

"For though there be that are called gods, whether in heaven or in earth, (as there be gods many, and lords many,)"

Paul acknowledges the existence of other deities that people may worship, whether in the heavens or on earth. In various cultures, there are many gods and lords that people may revere.

Verse 6:

"But to us, there is but one God, the Father, of whom are all things, and we in him; and one Lord Jesus Christ, by whom are all things, and we by him."

Paul underscores the unique perspective of Christians. To them, there is only one true God, the Father, from whom all things come, and one Lord Jesus Christ, through whom all things exist. This monotheistic view sets the Christian faith apart.

Verse 7:

"Howbeit, there is not in every man that knowledge: for some with conscience of the idol unto this hour eat it as a thing offered unto an idol, and their conscience being weak is defiled."

Paul acknowledges that not everyone possesses the same level of knowledge or understanding about the insignificance of idols. Some individuals, with a weak conscience, may still associate the food with idol worship when they eat it, and this can lead to a defiled conscience.

Verse 8:

"But meat commendeth us not to God: for neither, if we eat, are we the better; neither, if we eat not, are we the worse."

Paul clarifies that the act of eating or abstaining from food does not impact one's standing with God. It does not make a person better or worse in God's eyes. What matters is the heart and the motivation behind one's actions.

Verse 9:

"But take heed lest by any means this liberty of yours become a stumbling block to them that are weak."

Paul emphasizes the need for caution. While believers have the liberty to eat food sacrificed to idols with full knowledge of its insignificance, they must be careful not to cause weaker believers to stumble or be led into sin by their actions.

Verse 10:

"For if any man sees thee which hast knowledge sit at meat in the idol's temple, shall not the conscience of him which is weak be emboldened to eat those things which are offered to idols;"

Paul provides a practical example. If a knowledgeable believer is seen eating in an idol's temple, a weaker believer may be emboldened to do the same, even if it violates their conscience.

Verse 11:

"And through thy knowledge shall the weak brother perish, for whom Christ died?"

Paul underscores the serious consequences of causing a weaker believer to go against their conscience. It can lead to their spiritual harm or "perishing," despite the fact that Christ died for them.

Verse 12:

"But when ye sin so against the brethren and wound their weak conscience, ye sin against Christ."

Paul emphasizes that by causing a weaker believer to stumble and defile their conscience, it is not just a sin against that person but also a sin against Christ Himself. This underscores the gravity of the matter.

Verse 13:

"Wherefore, if meat make my brother to offend, I will eat no flesh while the world standeth, lest I make my brother to offend."

Paul concludes by stating his personal commitment to avoid eating meat if it would cause a weaker brother to stumble or be offended. He is willing to sacrifice his own liberty for the sake of the spiritual well-being of others. This demonstrates the principle of putting the welfare of fellow believers above personal freedom.

In 1 Corinthians 8:1-13, Paul addresses the issue of eating food sacrificed to idols. He emphasizes that knowledge should be accompanied by love and consideration for others. While idols are nothing, he cautions against causing weaker believers to stumble through one's actions. The central message is that love and concern for fellow believers should guide decisions, even when exercising personal liberty, to avoid causing harm to others' consciences.

CHAPTER 9

The Rights and Responsibilities of Apostles

The theme of 1 Corinthians chapter 9 is "The Rights and Responsibilities of Apostles." In this chapter, the Apostle Paul discusses his apostolic ministry and the principles of Christian service, using his own life and ministry as an example. The central theme revolves around the rights and responsibilities of those engaged in the work of spreading the Gospel. Here's an overview of the main themes and points in 1 Corinthians chapter 9:

1. Paul's Rights as an Apostle (1 Corinthians 9:1-14): Paul begins by asserting his rights as an apostle and defending his legitimacy as a servant of Christ. He explains that as an apostle, he has the right to

receive support for his work, including material provisions. He uses various examples, including the principle that those who work in the temple receive their livelihood from the temple, to support this claim.

2. For the Sake of the Gospel (1 Corinthians 9:15-23): Paul acknowledges that he willingly foregoes some of his rights and financial support to avoid hindering the preaching of the Gospel. He becomes "all things to all men" in order to win some to Christ. His primary motivation is the salvation of others and the advancement of the Gospel.

3. The Race of Faith (1 Corinthians 9:24-27): Paul uses the metaphor of an athlete in a race to illustrate the discipline and determination required in the Christian life. He encourages believers to run the race with purpose, self-control, and the goal of receiving an imperishable prize.

The central theme of 1 Corinthians chapter 9 is the balance between the rights of Christian workers, especially apostles, and their willingness to set aside those rights for the sake of the Gospel and the spiritual welfare of others. Paul's emphasis is on the sacrificial nature of Christian service and the importance of being flexible and adaptable in ministry for the greater purpose of spreading the message of Christ.

Verse 1:

"Am I not an apostle? am I not free? have I not seen Jesus Christ our Lord? are not ye my work in the Lord?"

Paul begins by addressing his apostleship. He asserts his authority and freedom in Christ. He reminds the Corinthians that he had a personal encounter with Jesus Christ, and he considers them as the fruit of his work in the Lord. This introduction sets the stage for his discussion about his rights as an apostle.

Verse 2:

"If I be not an apostle unto others, yet doubtless I am to you: for the seal of mine apostleship are ye in the Lord."

Paul acknowledges that there may be doubts about his apostleship among others, but he firmly asserts that he is undoubtedly an apostle to the Corinthians. He considers the Corinthians as a living proof or seal of his apostleship, indicating that his work among them is evidence of his apostolic calling.

Verse 3:

"Mine answer to them that do examine me is this,"

Paul anticipates that some may question or examine his apostleship. He is preparing to provide a response to their inquiries.

Verse 4:

"Have we not power to eat and to drink?"

Paul begins to discuss the rights and privileges that apostles have. He starts with the question of whether they have the authority to eat and drink. This implies that apostles have the right to be supported in their ministry by the community they serve.

Verse 5:

"Have we not power to lead about a sister, a wife, as well as other apostles, and as the brethren of the Lord, and Cephas?"

Paul continues to assert the apostles' rights, including the right to marry or have a wife accompany them in their ministry, as some other apostles, including Peter (Cephas), and the Lord's brothers do.

Verse 6:

"Or I only and Barnabas, have not we power to forbear working?"

Paul highlights his and Barnabas' position of not exercising certain rights. They chose not to receive financial support from the Corinthians and instead worked with their own hands to support themselves. This was a conscious choice to avoid any perceived hindrance to the gospel.

Verse 7:

"Who goeth a warfare any time at his own charges? who planteth a vineyard and eateth not of the fruit thereof? or who feedeth a flock and eateth not of the milk of the flock?"

Paul uses three analogies to illustrate his point. Just as a soldier doesn't bear the cost of his own warfare, a vineyard worker enjoys the fruit of his labor, and a shepherd partakes of the milk from his flock, so too should those who labor in the gospel receive support from their ministry.

Verse 8:

"Say I these things as a man? or saith not the law the same also?"

Paul reinforces his argument by referencing the principle found in the law. The Old Testament law also supported the idea that those who worked in the service of the Lord should receive their portion from it. This is a validation of the principle he's advocating.

Verse 9:

"For it is written in the law of Moses, Thou shalt not muzzle the mouth of the ox that treadeth out the corn. Doth God take care for oxen?"

Paul quotes a scriptural reference from Deuteronomy 25:4, which relates to the humane treatment of animals. He asks a rhetorical question, indicating that this principle is not primarily about caring for animals; rather, it illustrates a broader principle about supporting those who work.

Verse 10:

"Or saith he it altogether for our sakes? For our sakes, no doubt, this is written: that he that ploweth should plow in hope, and that he that thresheth in hope should be partaker of his hope."

Paul explains that the law's principle is intended for the benefit of human workers, not just animals. It teaches that those who work, like farmers plowing and threshing, should do so with the hope of sharing in the results of their labor. This is an argument for supporting those who labor in ministry, including apostles like himself.

In 1 Corinthians 9:1-10, Paul defends his apostleship and the rights of apostles. He argues that apostles have the right to receive support for their ministry, based on the principles found in the Old Testament law. He illustrates his point with analogies and emphasizes that these principles are primarily for the benefit of those who labor in the service of the Lord. Paul's aim is to address any questions or doubts about his apostleship and the legitimacy of his claims.

Verse 11:

"If we have sown unto you, spiritual things, is it a great thing if we shall reap your carnal things?"

Paul continues to defend his right to receive support for his ministry. He asks the Corinthians to consider the principle that if he and others have sown spiritual blessings and teachings among them, it is reasonable to expect that they, in turn, would provide material or financial support for their spiritual leaders.

Verse 12:

"If others be partakers of this power over you, are not we rather? Nevertheless, we have not used this power; but suffer all things, lest we should hinder the gospel of Christ."

Paul points out that other leaders or apostles who have ministered to the Corinthians have a similar right to receive support, but he and Barnabas have chosen not to use this right. They willingly endure hardships to avoid hindering the spread of the gospel, demonstrating their dedication to the mission.

Verse 13:

"Do ye not know that they which minister about holy things live of the things of the temple? and they which wait at the altar are partakers with the altar?"

Paul makes an analogy by referencing the practice of the Old Testament priesthood. Those who serve in the temple and at the altar are supported by the offerings brought to the altar. This illustrates the principle that those who serve in a sacred capacity should receive their livelihood from the ministry they perform.

Verse 14:

"Even so hath the Lord ordained that they which preach the gospel should live of the gospel."

Paul highlights that the Lord has established the principle that those who preach the gospel should receive their material support from the preaching of the gospel. This reinforces the idea that it is entirely appropriate for those in Christian ministry to be financially sustained through their work.

Verse 15:

"But I have used none of these things: neither have I written these things, that it should be so done unto me: for it were better for me to die than that any man should make my glorying void."

Paul emphasizes that he is not discussing these matters to personally benefit from them. He has not claimed his right to financial support, and he is not seeking to do so. Instead, he considers it more important to maintain his integrity and not hinder the gospel, even to the point of personal sacrifice.

Verse 16:

"For though I preach the gospel, I have nothing to glory of: for necessity is laid upon me; yea, woe is unto me if I preach not the gospel!"

Paul acknowledges that preaching the gospel is not a source of personal pride or glory for him. He feels a sense of necessity and duty to proclaim the gospel, and he regards it as a solemn responsibility. He is compelled to preach the gospel, and the consequences of failing to do so would be dire.

Verse 17:

"For if I do this thing willingly, I have a reward: but if against my will, a dispensation of the gospel is committed unto me."

Paul contrasts preaching willingly with doing it against his will. If he preaches willingly, he will have a reward. However, even if he were to do it against his own inclination, the responsibility of sharing the gospel has been entrusted to him as a divine dispensation or stewardship.

Verse 18:

"What is my reward then? Verily that, when I preach the gospel, I may make the gospel of Christ without charge, that I abuse not my power in the gospel."

Paul's ultimate reward is to preach the gospel without charge, to offer the message of Christ freely without demanding support from those he ministers to. This approach avoids the misuse of his authority in the gospel and keeps the focus on the message itself.

Verse 19:

"For though I be free from all men, yet have I made myself servant unto all, that I might gain the more."

Paul emphasizes his freedom in Christ, yet he willingly chooses to become a servant to all. His motivation is to win more people to Christ, showing his willingness to adapt his approach for the sake of the gospel.

Verse 20:

"And unto the Jews, I became as a Jew, that I might gain the Jews; to them that are under the law, as under the law, that I might gain them that are under the law;"

Paul illustrates his adaptability by explaining that he adjusts his behavior and approach based on the cultural or religious background of his audience. When ministering to Jews, he becomes like a Jew in his practices and customs to connect with them.

In 1 Corinthians 9:11-20, Paul continues to discuss his right to financial support as an apostle and the principle that those who preach the gospel should be supported by it. He emphasizes his willingness to endure hardships and not make use of this right for the sake of the gospel. He highlights his sense of obligation to preach the gospel and his adaptability to reach different groups of people effectively. Paul's primary concern is the spread of the gospel, and he is ready to adapt his approach and sacrifice personal benefits for the sake of this mission.

Verse 21:

"To them that are without law, as without law, (being not without law to God, but under the law to Christ,) that I might gain them that are without law."

Paul continues his discussion on adaptability in his ministry. He explains that when he interacts with those who are not bound by the Jewish law (Gentiles), he adapts to their ways (within the bounds of moral and ethical conduct), not being overly rigid. However, he makes it clear that he remains under the law of Christ, meaning he still follows the teachings and principles of Christ.

Verse 22:

"To the weak became I as weak, that I might gain the weak: I am made all things to all men, that I might by all means save some."

Paul's adaptability extends to those who are weak or vulnerable in their faith. He meets them where they are, understanding their struggles and concerns. His goal is to reach and save as many people as possible, and he is willing to adjust his approach to achieve this.
Verse 23:

"And this I do for the gospel's sake, that I might be partaker thereof with you."

Paul's adaptability is motivated by his commitment to the gospel. He is willing to do whatever it takes to share the good news of Christ. He desires to be a partaker of the blessings of the gospel alongside those he ministers to.
Verse 24:

"Know ye not that they which run in a race run all, but one receiveth the prize? So run, that ye may obtain."

Paul draws an analogy to a footrace. In a race, all runners compete, but only one receives the prize. He encourages the Corinthians to run their spiritual race with the same determination and commitment, striving to obtain the prize of eternal life.
Verse 25:

"And every man that striveth for the mastery is temperate in all things. Now they do it to obtain a corruptible crown, but we an incorruptible."

Paul highlights the discipline required for those striving for mastery or success. Athletes exercise self-control and discipline in their training. He contrasts the temporary rewards in earthly races (corruptible crowns) with the eternal reward that Christians are striving for (an incorruptible crown, symbolizing eternal life).
Verse 26:

"I therefore so run, not as uncertainly; so, fight I, not as one that beateth the air:"

Paul emphasizes that he does not run the spiritual race uncertainly or aimlessly. He does not engage in spiritual warfare haphazardly. His actions are purposeful and focused.
Verse 27:

"But I keep under my body and bring it into subjection, lest that by any means, when I have preached to others, I myself should be a castaway."

Paul underscores the importance of self-discipline. He subjects his own body and desires to control. This self-discipline is to prevent the possibility of being disqualified or becoming a castaway, despite having preached to others. He recognizes the need to live a life consistent with his preaching to avoid hypocrisy and falling away from the faith.

In 1 Corinthians 9:21-27, Paul continues to stress his adaptability in ministry, emphasizing his commitment to reaching as many people as possible for the sake of the gospel. He uses the analogy of a race to encourage the Corinthians to run their spiritual race with determination, seeking the eternal reward. He also highlights the importance of self-discipline to avoid hypocrisy and falling away from the faith, despite being an effective preacher to others. Paul's dedication to the gospel and his adaptability are central themes in this passage.

C H A P T E R 1 0

Avoiding Idolatry and Temptation

The theme of 1 Corinthians chapter 10 is "Avoiding Idolatry and Temptation." In this chapter, the Apostle Paul addresses the issue of food offered to idols, the importance of avoiding idolatry, and the temptations that believers may face in their daily lives. The central theme revolves around the need for Christians to remain faithful to God and avoid compromising their faith by engaging in practices associated with idolatry. Here's an overview of the main themes and points in 1 Corinthians chapter 10:

1. Warnings from Israel's History (1 Corinthians 10:1-13): Paul begins by reminding the Corinthians of the experiences of the Israelites in the wilderness. He highlights that although they had received blessings and deliverance, many of them fell into idolatry and faced consequences. Paul uses this history as a warning to the Corinthians, encouraging them to learn from these examples and to avoid idolatry and sinful behaviors.

2. Freedom to Eat, but with Caution (1 Corinthians 10:14-22): Paul addresses the issue of food offered to idols. He emphasizes that Christians have the freedom to eat whatever is sold in the marketplace without questioning its origin. However, he warns against participating in idolatrous rituals or partaking in meals in idol temples. He highlights that Christians cannot partake of the Lord's table and the table of demons simultaneously.

3. Avoiding Offense and Seeking Others' Welfare (1 Corinthians 10:23-33): Paul underscores the importance of seeking the welfare of others, both believers and non-believers, in the exercise of Christian liberties. He advises that if eating a particular food would cause someone else to stumble or misunderstand, it's better to abstain for the sake of their conscience. He emphasizes that everything should be done for the glory of God.

The central theme in 1 Corinthians chapter 10 is the need for believers to avoid idolatry, temptation, and compromising their faith while living in a society with various practices and beliefs. Paul encourages Christians to exercise their freedom responsibly, seeking the welfare of others and glorifying God in all they do. The chapter serves as a guide for navigating potential pitfalls and challenges related to faith and cultural practices.

Verse 1:

"Moreover, brethren, I would not that ye should be ignorant, how that all our fathers were under the cloud, and all passed through the sea;"

Paul begins by addressing the Corinthians as brethren and expresses his desire that they should not be ignorant of certain historical events. He references the Israelites' journey in the wilderness when they were led by a cloud and miraculously crossed the Red Sea during the time of Moses.

Verse 2:

"And were all baptized unto Moses in the cloud and in the sea;"

Paul metaphorically describes the Israelites' experience as a baptism unto Moses. The cloud and the sea symbolize the protective and transformative work of God, as the Israelites passed through these elements under His guidance.

Verse 3:

"And did all eat the same spiritual meat;"

Paul refers to the manna that God provided to sustain the Israelites in the wilderness as "spiritual meat." This manna was a miraculous provision and a type of God's care for His people.

Verse 4:

"And did all drink the same spiritual drink: for they drank of that spiritual Rock that followed them: and that Rock was Christ."

Paul underscores that the Israelites also drank a spiritual drink from a spiritual Rock that followed them. This spiritual Rock is interpreted by Paul to represent Christ, highlighting the presence of Christ with the Israelites during their wilderness journey.

Verse 5:

"But with many of them, God was not well pleased: for they were overthrown in the wilderness."

Despite these remarkable blessings and spiritual experiences, many of the Israelites did not find favor with God. They rebelled and faced consequences, including being overthrown or perishing in the wilderness.

Verse 6:

"Now, these things were our examples, to the intent we should not lust after evil things, as they also lusted."

Paul emphasizes that the Israelites' experiences serve as examples and lessons for the Corinthian believers. They are meant to discourage the desire for evil things, warning against the same kinds of sinful desires that led to the Israelites' disobedience.

Verse 7:

"Neither be ye idolaters, as were some of them; as it is written, the people sat down to eat and drink and rose up to play."

Paul refers to the idolatry that some of the Israelites practiced, which involved engaging in pagan revelry, including eating and drinking, and engaging in immoral activities. He cites an incident from Exodus 32:6 when the Israelites worshiped the golden calf.

Verse 8:

"Neither let us commit fornication, as some of them committed and fell in one day three and twenty thousand."

Paul warns against the sin of sexual immorality, citing an incident from Numbers 25:1-9 when the Israelites engaged in fornication and faced severe consequences, including a plague that killed twenty-three thousand people in a single day.

Verse 9:

"Neither let us tempt Christ, as some of them also tempted and were destroyed of serpents."

Paul admonishes against testing or tempting Christ, referencing an event from Numbers 21:4-6 when the Israelites grumbled and complained, and God sent serpents among them as a punishment.
Verse 10:

"Neither murmur ye, as some of them also murmured and were destroyed of the destroyer."

Paul encourages the Corinthians not to grumble or complain as the Israelites did in the wilderness. When they murmured, God sent a destroyer among them to punish their discontent.

In 1 Corinthians 10:1-10, Paul draws parallels between the experiences of the Israelites in the wilderness and the spiritual lessons for the Corinthian believers. He highlights the importance of learning from the Israelites' mistakes, emphasizing the need to avoid idolatry, fornication, testing Christ, and murmuring. These historical examples serve as warnings about the consequences of disobedience and unfaithfulness to God.
Verse 11:

"Now, all these things happened unto them for ensamples: and they are written for our admonition, upon whom the ends of the world are come."

Paul emphasizes that the events and experiences of the Israelites in the wilderness serve as examples and warnings for Christians. The stories from the Old Testament are recorded for the benefit of believers, especially those who live in the latter times, to learn from their mistakes and experiences.
Verse 12:

"Wherefore let him that thinketh he standeth take heed lest he fall."

Paul issues a caution to believers who are confident in their faith. He warns them not to be overconfident or presumptuous about their spiritual standing, as even the Israelites who had witnessed God's miracles fell into sin and disobedience.

Verse 13:

"There hath no temptation taken you but such as is common to man: but God is faithful, who will not suffer you to be tempted above that ye are able; but will with the temptation also make a way to escape, that ye may be able to bear it."

Paul offers comfort and encouragement by assuring the Corinthians that the trials and temptations they face are not unique. They are common human experiences. God is faithful and will not allow them to be tempted beyond their ability to withstand. He promises to provide a way of escape so that they can endure and overcome temptation.

Verse 14:

"Wherefore, my dearly beloved, flee from idolatry."

Paul addresses the Corinthians affectionately as dearly beloved. He urges them to avoid idolatry, emphasizing the need to stay away from the worship of false gods and idols.

Verse 15:

"I speak as to wise men; judge ye what I say."

Paul appeals to the Corinthians' wisdom and judgment. He encourages them to carefully consider and evaluate his words, recognizing the importance of his message.

Verse 16:

"The cup of blessing which we bless, is it not the communion of the blood of Christ? The bread which we break, is it not the communion of the body of Christ?"

Paul introduces the concept of the Lord's Supper (communion) and highlights the profound significance of the elements. The cup and the bread are symbolic of the blood and body of

Christ, representing the shared fellowship and remembrance of Christ's sacrifice in the communion.

Verse 17:

"For we being many are one bread, and one body: for we are all partakers of that one bread."

Paul underscores the unity of believers in the body of Christ. When they partake of the same bread, they symbolize their oneness as a single body, emphasizing the communal aspect of the Lord's Supper.

Verse 18:

"Behold Israel after the flesh: are not they which eat of the sacrifices partakers of the altar?"

Paul draws a parallel with the Israelites who participate in the sacrifices offered at the altar. Just as they partake in the offerings, believers partake in the elements of the Lord's Supper, signifying their spiritual connection and fellowship with God.

Verse 19:

"What say I then? that the idol is anything, or that which is offered in sacrifice to idols is anything?"

Paul revisits the issue of idolatry. He questions whether idols themselves have any real significance or power, and whether the meat offered to idols retains any special quality after being sacrificed.

Verse 20:

"But I say, that the things which the Gentiles sacrifice, they sacrifice to devils and not to God: and I would not that ye should have fellowship with devils."

Paul clarifies that the sacrifices made by the Gentiles in pagan rituals are not offered to God but to demonic entities. He strongly advises the Corinthians against participating in or having fellowship with such practices and entities, emphasizing the importance of avoiding idolatry.

In 1 Corinthians 10:11-20, Paul continues to draw lessons from the Israelites' experiences in the wilderness, underscoring their relevance for the Corinthians. He warns against overconfidence in one's faith, encourages believers to flee from idolatry, and highlights the significance of the Lord's Supper as a symbol of unity and fellowship with Christ and fellow believers. Paul firmly advises against any involvement with idolatrous practices and the entities associated with them. These principles are meant to guide the Corinthians in their Christian walk and worship.

Verse 21:

"Ye cannot drink the cup of the Lord, and the cup of devils: ye cannot be partakers of the Lord's table, and of the table of devils."

Paul issues a strong warning to the Corinthians. He emphasizes the incompatibility of participating in both the Lord's table, symbolizing communion with Christ, and pagan rituals involving idols and demons. Believers cannot simultaneously maintain fellowship with God and engage in idolatry.

Verse 22:

"Do we provoke the Lord to jealousy? are we stronger than he?"

Paul questions whether the Corinthians are provoking the jealousy of the Lord by attempting to have both Christian fellowship and idolatrous practices. He emphasizes that they are not stronger or more powerful than God, and such behavior challenges His rightful authority.

Verse 23:

"All things are lawful for me, but all things are not expedient: all things are lawful for me, but all things edify not."

Paul reiterates the principle of Christian liberty. While believers have freedom in Christ, not everything is beneficial or edifying. Some actions, even if allowed, may not contribute to spiritual growth or the well-being of others.

Verse 24:

"Let no man seek his own, but every man another's wealth."

Paul encourages believers to prioritize the welfare of others over their own interests. Instead of seeking personal gain or benefit, they should focus on promoting the well-being and spiritual growth of fellow believers.

Verse 25:

"Whatsoever is sold in the shambles, that eat, asking no question for conscience's sake:"

Paul addresses the issue of purchasing meat in the marketplace, which may have been previously offered to idols. He advises the Corinthians to buy and eat such meat without raising questions of conscience, acknowledging that idols have no real significance.

Verse 26:

"For the earth is the Lord's, and the fullness thereof."

Paul reminds the Corinthians that everything in the world belongs to the Lord. Therefore, they can partake of His provisions with a clear conscience.

Verse 27:

"If any of them that believe not bid you to a feast, and ye be disposed to go; whatsoever is set before you, eat, asking no question for conscience's sake."

Paul advises that if unbelievers invite believers to a meal, and the believers are willing to attend, they should eat whatever is served without questioning its origin in case it has been sacrificed to idols. This approach avoids unnecessary offense or conflict.

Verse 28:

"But if any man says unto you, This is offered in sacrifice unto idols, eat not for his sake that showed it, and for conscience's sake: for the earth is the Lord's, and the fullness thereof."

However, if someone informs the believer that the food has been offered to idols, Paul advises refraining from eating it. This is not due to the idol's significance but out of consideration for the other person's conscience and to avoid causing offense.

Verse 29:

"Conscience, I say, not thine own, but of the other: for why is my liberty judged of another man's conscience?"

Paul reiterates that the concern is not about one's own conscience but the conscience of the other person. He questions why his liberty should be evaluated or criticized by someone else's conscience.

Verse 30:

"For if I by grace be a partaker, why am I evil spoken of for that for which I give thanks?"

Paul points out that if he, by God's grace, partakes of something and gives thanks, why should he be criticized for what he eats?

Verse 31:

"Whether, therefore, ye eat or drink, or whatsoever ye do, do all to the glory of God."

Paul's central message is that in all things, including eating and drinking, believers should act in a manner that brings glory to God. Their actions should reflect their faith and honor God.

Verse 32:

"Give none offense, neither to the Jews, nor to the Gentiles, nor to the church of God:"

Paul emphasizes the importance of avoiding actions that may cause offense to Jews, Gentiles, or fellow believers in the church. He highlights the need for sensitivity to different cultural and spiritual backgrounds.

Verse 33:

"Even as I please all men in all things, not seeking mine own profit, but the profit of many, that they may be saved."

Paul concludes by sharing his own example. He seeks to please everyone by not pursuing his own advantage but rather the benefit and salvation of others. His actions are driven by a deep concern for the spiritual welfare of those he interacts with.

In 1 Corinthians 10:21-33, Paul continues to address the Corinthians' participation in idolatrous practices and the use of meat sacrificed to idols. He underscores the incompatibility of fellowship with Christ and participation in idol worship. While emphasizing Christian liberty, he also stresses the importance of considering the conscience of others and prioritizing the glory of God and the welfare of fellow believers in all actions and decisions. Paul's teachings aim to promote unity, sensitivity, and the spiritual well-being of the Corinthian church.

CHAPTER 11

Proper Conduct in Worship and the Lord's Supper

The theme of 1 Corinthians chapter 11 is "Proper Conduct in Worship and the Lord's Supper." In this chapter, the Apostle Paul addresses the Corinthians' behavior during public worship gatherings and provides instructions regarding the observance of the Lord's Supper. The central theme revolves around the importance of maintaining reverence and order in worship, particularly during the celebration of the Eucharist. Here's an overview of the main themes and points in 1 Corinthians chapter 11:

1. Head Coverings and Gender Distinction (1 Corinthians 11:1-16): Paul begins by discussing the issue of head coverings in the worship assembly. He emphasizes that men should pray and prophesy with uncovered heads, as they represent the glory of God. In contrast, women should have their heads covered as a symbol of submission, recognizing the divine order in creation.

2. The Lord's Supper (1 Corinthians 11:17-34): Paul addresses the disorder and irreverence that the Corinthians have displayed during the observance of the Lord's Supper. He reminds them of the significance of this sacrament, emphasizing the need for self-examination and discerning the body of Christ. He warns against partaking in an unworthy manner, recognizing the consequences of doing so.

3. Concern for Unity and Shared Meals (1 Corinthians 11:33-34): Paul instructs the Corinthians to wait for one another when coming together for the Lord's Supper, ensuring that it is observed as a shared communal meal rather than a divisive and self-indulgent practice.

The central theme in 1 Corinthians chapter 11 is the need for order, reverence, and proper conduct in public worship, especially during the celebration of the Lord's Supper. Paul emphasizes the importance of recognizing the roles and distinctions between genders and the significance of partaking in the Eucharist with a proper attitude and understanding. The chapter provides guidance for conducting worship services in a manner that honors God and promotes unity among believers.

Verse 1:

"Be ye followers of me, even as I also am of Christ."

Paul begins by urging the Corinthians to imitate him as he follows Christ. He sees himself as an example of Christian living, encouraging them to model their behavior after his example in following Christ.

Verse 2:

"Now I praise you, brethren, that ye remember me in all things and keep the ordinances, as I delivered them to you."

Paul commends the Corinthians for remembering and maintaining the ordinances or teachings he delivered to them. He is pleased that they have retained these instructions.

Verse 3:

"But I would have you know that the head of every man is Christ, and the head of the woman is the man, and the head of Christ is God."

Paul establishes a hierarchical order of authority. Christ is the head of every man, man is the head of woman, and God is the head of Christ. This structure reflects roles and submission in Christian relationships.

Verse 4:

"Every man praying or prophesying, having his head covered, dishonoureth his head."

Paul addresses the practice of men covering their heads while praying or prophesying. He asserts that this dishonors their head, which is Christ. It is important to note that the specifics of this practice might have cultural context in Corinth.

Verse 5:

"But every woman that prayeth or prophesieth with her head uncovered dishonoureth her head, for that is even all one as if she were shaven."

Paul also addresses women, explaining that if a woman prays or prophesies without her head covered, it dishonors her head, which is the man. The imagery of being shaven suggests a loss of distinction and a disregard for cultural norms.

Verse 6:

"For if the woman be not covered, let her also be shorn: but if it be a shame for a woman to be shorn or shaven, let her be covered."

Paul presents a conditional statement. If a woman chooses not to be covered while praying or prophesying, then she might as well be shorn (have her hair cut short). However, he acknowledges that such a practice is considered shameful for women, so he recommends that they cover their heads instead.

Verse 7:

"For a man indeed ought not to cover his head, forasmuch as he is the image and glory of God: but the woman is the glory of the man."

Paul offers reasons for these instructions. Men should not cover their heads because they are created in the image and glory of God. In contrast, women are the glory of men. These distinctions reflect the order established by God.

Verse 8:

"For the man is not of the woman, but the woman of the man."

Paul reinforces the hierarchical relationship, noting that man was not created from woman, but woman was created from man. This highlights the order of creation in which man was created first.

Verse 9:

"Neither was the man created for the woman, but the woman for the man."

Paul further emphasizes that woman was created for man, suggesting that her creation was for the purpose of being a suitable helper or companion to the man.

Verse 10:

"For this cause ought the woman to have power on her head because of the angels."

Paul concludes this section by asserting that women should have a symbol of authority on their heads, likely referring to head coverings, because of the angels. The reference to angels and their role in observing Christian worship is somewhat obscure and has led to various interpretations.

In 1 Corinthians 11:1-10, Paul addresses issues related to the behavior of men and women in the context of Christian worship. He establishes a hierarchical order of authority in which Christ is the head of every man, man is the head of woman, and God is the head of Christ. He also discusses the practice of head coverings for women, emphasizing the reasons for these practices based on the order of creation and Christian customs. The concept of angels observing worship adds a layer of mystery to this passage. Paul's instructions are intended to reflect a sense of order and respect within the Christian community during worship.

Verse 11:

"Nevertheless, neither is the man without the woman, neither the woman without the man, in the Lord."

Paul introduces a balance to his previous statements about the hierarchy within marriage. He emphasizes that within the context of the Lord (in the spiritual realm), men and women are interdependent. In the Lord, neither gender is exclusive or self-sufficient; they complement and need each other.

Verse 12:

"For as the woman is of the man, even so is the man also by the woman, but all things of God."

Paul continues to underline the interdependence of men and women. Women came from men (Eve was created from Adam), but men are also born of women through childbirth. Ultimately, both men and women, along with their respective roles, have their origin in God. Verse 13:

"Judge in yourselves: is it comely that a woman prays unto God uncovered?"

Paul challenges the Corinthians to use their own judgment. He raises the question of whether it is appropriate for a woman to pray to God without a head covering. He encourages them to consider the cultural norms and appropriateness in their context.
Verse 14:

"Doth not even nature itself teach you that if a man has long hair, it is a shame unto him?"

Paul introduces the idea that nature teaches a distinction between men and women. In many cultures, long hair has traditionally been associated with femininity, and Paul suggests that it is considered inappropriate for a man to have long hair.
Verse 15:

"But if a woman has long hair, it is a glory to her: for her hair is given her for a covering."

Conversely, Paul highlights that for women, long hair is considered a glory and is given to her as a natural covering. This suggests that the Corinthians should take into account the cultural and social norms of their time when deciding whether women should wear an additional head covering during prayer or worship.

In 1 Corinthians 11:11-15, Paul addresses the interdependence of men and women in the spiritual realm, emphasizing their mutual need for one another. He encourages the Corinthians to use their judgment when considering whether women should have head coverings during prayer and worship. Paul introduces the idea that cultural norms and the distinction between men and women, as indicated by long hair, should be taken into account. Ultimately, he emphasizes the need for appropriateness and cultural sensitivity in their worship practices.

Verse 16:

"But if any man seems to be contentious, we have no such custom, neither the churches of God."

Paul addresses the possibility of contention or dispute regarding the issue of head coverings. He asserts that such a custom or practice is not found in the churches of God. This statement implies that the practice of head coverings may not be universal among Christian congregations and is not a fundamental doctrine.

Verse 17:

"Now in this that I declare unto you I praise you not, that ye come together not for the better, but for the worse."

Paul expresses his displeasure with the Corinthians' behavior when they gather as a church. He believes that their gatherings have a negative rather than a positive impact. This may refer to their divisions, conflicts, and misunderstandings about worship practices, including head coverings.

Verse 18:

"For first of all, when ye come together in the church, I hear that there be divisions among you, and I partly believe it."

Paul confirms that he has heard about the divisions and disputes within the Corinthian church when they assemble. He acknowledges the existence of these issues, though he doesn't fully trust all the reports he's received.

Verse 19:

"For there must be also heresies among you, that they which are approved may be made manifest among you."

Paul acknowledges that some level of disagreement or heresies may exist within the church. He suggests that these disagreements serve a purpose – to reveal and test those who are genuinely approved or faithful in their beliefs.

Verse 20:

"When ye come together, therefore, into one place, this is not to eat the Lord's supper."

Paul points out that when the Corinthians gather in one place for worship, their primary purpose should not be to simply eat a meal resembling the Lord's Supper (communion). The divisions and issues within the church have undermined the true significance of their gatherings.

In 1 Corinthians 11:16-20, Paul confronts the problem of contention and divisions within the Corinthian church, particularly concerning the issue of head coverings. He expresses his disappointment in the way they come together, highlighting that their divisions negatively impact their gatherings. Paul also recognizes that some level of disagreement is inevitable but suggests it serves to reveal the genuine believers. He emphasizes that their gatherings should primarily be for the purpose of observing the Lord's Supper with reverence and unity.

Verse 20:

"When ye come together, therefore, into one place, this is not to eat the Lord's supper."

Paul reiterates the point he made earlier, emphasizing that when the Corinthians gather as a church, their primary purpose should not be to eat a common meal. The context is crucial here as he addresses their divisions and issues in the church.

Verse 21:

"For in eating every one taketh before other his own supper: and one is hungry, and another is drunken."

Paul highlights the problem with their gatherings. Instead of partaking in a solemn and reverent observance of the Lord's Supper, some individuals are selfishly consuming their own meals. This has led to inequities, with some going hungry while others overindulge in food and drink.

Verse 22:

"What? Have ye not houses to eat and to drink in? Or despise ye the church of God and shame them that have not? What shall I say to you? Shall I praise you in this? I praise you not."

Paul questions the Corinthians' behavior. He asks whether they don't have their own homes to eat and drink in and criticizes them for treating the church gatherings with contempt. He points out that their actions shame those who have less. He is clearly not praising their conduct in this matter.

Verse 23:

"For I have received of the Lord that which also I delivered unto you, That the Lord Jesus the same night in which he was betrayed took bread:"

Paul shifts the focus to the Lord's Supper itself, explaining that he received this teaching from the Lord and passed it on to the Corinthians. He refers to the specific event when Jesus, on the night of His betrayal, took bread.

Verse 24:

"And when he had given thanks, he break it and said, Take, eat; this is my body, which is broken for you: this do in remembrance of me."

Paul describes the actions of Jesus during the Last Supper. Jesus gave thanks, broke the bread, and instructed His disciples to eat it,

explaining that it represents His body, which was broken for them. He urged them to observe this act in remembrance of Him.
Verse 25:

"After the same manner also he took the cup, when he had supped, saying, This cup is the new testament in my blood: this do ye, as oft as ye drink it, in remembrance of me."

Paul continues by narrating Jesus' actions during the Last Supper. After supper, Jesus took the cup and explained that it symbolized the new covenant in His blood. He instructed His disciples to drink it in remembrance of Him, highlighting the importance of commemorating His sacrifice through the Lord's Supper.

In 1 Corinthians 11:20-25, Paul addresses the Corinthians' improper behavior during their gatherings, specifically regarding the Lord's Supper. He emphasizes the need for reverence and unity during the observance of the Lord's Supper. He recounts the actions of Jesus during the Last Supper, highlighting the significance of the bread and the cup as symbols of His body and blood, urging the Corinthians to observe this act in remembrance of Him. Paul's aim is to redirect their focus toward the sacred nature of the Lord's Supper and away from their divisive and selfish practices.
Verse 26:

"For as often as ye eat this bread and drink this cup, ye do show the Lord's death till he come."

Paul emphasizes the ongoing nature of the Lord's Supper, suggesting that believers should regularly partake of the bread and cup. This practice serves as a continual testimony to the Lord's death until His return. It symbolizes their remembrance and proclamation of Christ's sacrificial death and the expectation of His second coming.
Verse 27:

"Wherefore whosoever shall eat this bread and drink this cup of the Lord unworthily, shall be guilty of the body and blood of the Lord."

Paul issues a solemn warning regarding the manner in which one should approach the Lord's Supper. Those who partake of the bread and cup in an unworthy or irreverent manner are held responsible for treating Christ's body and blood with disrespect.

Verse 28:

"But let a man examine himself, and so let him eat of that bread and drink of that cup."

Paul encourages believers to engage in self-examination before partaking in the Lord's Supper. This self-examination involves introspection, reflection on one's relationship with God, and addressing any unconfessed sin. Only after such examination should one partake in the elements.

Verse 29:

"For he that eateth and drinketh unworthily, eateth and drinketh damnation to himself, not discerning the Lord's body."

Continuing the warning, Paul explains that eating and drinking the elements in an unworthy manner leads to self-condemnation. This occurs when individuals fail to recognize or discern the significance of the Lord's body in the observance of the Supper.

Verse 30:

"For this cause many are weak and sickly among you, and many sleep."

Paul points out the consequences of unworthy participation in the Lord's Supper. Some Corinthians have experienced weakness, illness, and even death. These afflictions serve as divine discipline for their irreverence and lack of discernment.

Verse 31:

"For if we would judge ourselves, we should not be judged."

Paul offers a remedy: by examining themselves and addressing their own shortcomings, believers can avoid divine judgment.

Verse 32:

"But when we are judged, we are chastened of the Lord, that we should not be condemned with the world."

Paul explains that if believers do not engage in self-judgment and correction, the Lord may discipline them to prevent their condemnation along with the world. Divine chastening, in this context, serves as a means of correction and protection.

Verse 33:

"Wherefore, my brethren, when ye come together to eat, tarry one for another."

Paul advises the Corinthians to be considerate of one another when they gather for the Lord's Supper. They should wait for one another and not rush through the meal. This emphasizes the communal and relational aspects of the observance.

Verse 34:

"And if any man hunger, let him eat at home; that ye come not together unto condemnation. And the rest will I set in order when I come."

Paul suggests that if someone is hungry, they should eat at home rather than treating the Lord's Supper as a common meal. By doing so, the Corinthians can avoid coming together for the Lord's Supper in a manner that leads to condemnation. Paul indicates his intention to address other matters when he visits them, underlining that the issues concerning the Lord's Supper require immediate attention.

In 1 Corinthians 11:26-34, Paul concludes his teaching on the Lord's Supper by stressing its ongoing significance as a testimony to Christ's death and His return. He warns against unworthy participation, encouraging self-examination and recognition of the Lord's body. Paul highlights the consequences of irreverent participation but also underscores the potential for self-correction through self-judgment. He advises the Corinthians to wait for one another and to approach the Supper with consideration for others. The observance of the Lord's Supper should be a solemn and reverent act of worship, not a common meal. Paul plans to address further issues in person, indicating the importance of proper observance of the Lord's Supper.

CHAPTER 12

Spiritual Gifts and the Unity of the Body

The theme of 1 Corinthians chapter 12 is "Spiritual Gifts and the Unity of the Body." In this chapter, the Apostle Paul addresses the topic of spiritual gifts and their role within the body of Christ, emphasizing the unity and interdependence of believers in the church. Here's an overview of the main themes and points in 1 Corinthians chapter 12:

1. Diversity of Spiritual Gifts (1 Corinthians 12:1-11): Paul begins by discussing the various spiritual gifts given by the Holy Spirit to believers. He emphasizes that these gifts are manifestations of the

Spirit and are given for the common good. The diversity of gifts highlights the uniqueness and interdependence of the members of the body of Christ.

2. One Body, Many Members (1 Corinthians 12:12-26): Paul uses the analogy of the human body to illustrate the unity and diversity within the church. Just as a body has many parts, each with its own function, so does the body of Christ. All members are essential, and their differences contribute to the overall health and functioning of the body.

3. The Hierarchy of Spiritual Gifts (1 Corinthians 12:27-31): Paul discusses the roles and functions of various gifts in the church. He emphasizes that not all believers have the same gifts, and some gifts are more critical than others. He encourages believers to earnestly desire the greater gifts while also affirming the value of love as the most excellent way.

The central theme in 1 Corinthians chapter 12 is the recognition and understanding of spiritual gifts and their role in promoting the unity and functionality of the body of Christ. Paul emphasizes that each believer has a unique contribution to make, and no one should consider themselves more or less important than others. The chapter underscores the importance of mutual dependence and the pursuit of love and unity within the church.

Verse 1:

"Now concerning spiritual gifts, brethren, I would not have you ignorant."

Paul begins this chapter by addressing the topic of spiritual gifts. He doesn't want the Corinthians to be uninformed or ignorant about the various gifts that the Holy Spirit bestows upon believers.

Verse 2:

"Ye know that ye were Gentiles, carried away unto these dumb idols, even as ye were led."

Paul reminds the Corinthians of their past as Gentiles who were led to worship idols that could not speak or provide real guidance. He contrasts this with the spiritual gifts that come from the living God.

Verse 3:

"Wherefore I give you to understand that no man speaking by the Spirit of God calleth Jesus accursed: and that no man can say that Jesus is the Lord but by the Holy Ghost."

Paul emphasizes the importance of recognizing that anyone speaking by the Spirit of God will not speak against Jesus. On the contrary, it is only by the Holy Spirit that one can genuinely confess Jesus as Lord. This underscores the divine origin of genuine spiritual experiences.

Verse 4:

"Now there are diversities of gifts, but the same Spirit."

Paul acknowledges that there is a diversity of spiritual gifts, but they all come from the same Holy Spirit. This highlights the unity within the Trinity and the diversity of spiritual manifestations.

Verse 5:

"And there are differences of administrations, but the same Lord."

Paul notes that there are various ways that these spiritual gifts can be administered or used, but they all come from the same Lord, referring to Jesus Christ. This emphasizes the variety of roles and ministries within the body of Christ.

Verse 6:

"And there are diversities of operations, but it is the same God which worketh all in all."

Paul further underscores the diversity of ways in which these spiritual gifts operate. However, he emphasizes that it is the same God who is behind all of these workings in and through believers. This emphasizes the divine source of all spiritual activity.

Verse 7:

"But the manifestation of the Spirit is given to every man to profit withal."

Paul emphasizes that the purpose of spiritual gifts is not for personal gain or glory but for the common good. The Spirit's manifestations are given to benefit the entire body of believers, fostering unity and edification.

Verse 8:

"For to one is given by the Spirit the word of wisdom; to another the word of knowledge by the same Spirit;"

Paul begins to list specific spiritual gifts. The first two mentioned are the "word of wisdom" and the "word of knowledge." These gifts involve divine insight and understanding, which can be used to impart wisdom and knowledge to others within the church.

Verse 9:

"To another faith by the same Spirit; to another the gifts of healing by the same Spirit;"

Paul continues with other gifts. One is given the gift of faith, indicating a special ability to trust in God's power and promises. Another is given the gifts of healing, enabling them to pray for and see healing miracles through the Holy Spirit.

Verse 10:

"To another the working of miracles; to another prophecy; to another discerning of spirits; to another divers kinds of tongues; to another the interpretation of tongues."

Paul completes the list of spiritual gifts. Some are granted the ability to work miracles, while others are given the gift of prophecy, discerning of spirits, speaking in different kinds of tongues (languages), and interpreting tongues. These gifts are diverse and serve various purposes within the body of believers.

In 1 Corinthians 12:1-10, Paul introduces the topic of spiritual gifts and emphasizes the importance of understanding their source and purpose. He clarifies that these gifts come from the Holy Spirit, Jesus Christ, and God, highlighting the unity within the Trinity. Paul lists several specific spiritual gifts, each with a unique function, all intended for the common good and edification of the church. These gifts are part of the broader spiritual landscape within the Christian community, contributing to its diversity and unity.

Verse 11:

"But all these worketh that one and the selfsame Spirit, dividing to every man severally as he will."

Paul emphasizes that all of these spiritual gifts are activated by the same Holy Spirit. The Spirit distributes these gifts individually to believers according to His will. This underscores that spiritual gifts are not earned or acquired but are given by God's sovereign choice.

Verse 12:

"For as the body is one and hath many members, and all the members of that one body, being many, are one body: so also, is Christ."

Paul draws an analogy between the unity of the body and the unity of Christ, which is the church. Just as a human body is composed of many parts but functions as one, so is the body of Christ. Believers, though diverse in their spiritual gifts and roles, form a single unified entity, which is the body of Christ.

Verse 13:

"For by one Spirit are we all baptized into one body, whether we be Jews or Gentiles, whether we be bond or free, and have been all made to drink into one Spirit."

Paul highlights the unifying work of the Holy Spirit. It is through the Holy Spirit that believers, regardless of their background or social status (Jews or Gentiles, bond or free), are baptized into one body, which is the body of Christ. This spiritual baptism and indwelling of the Spirit unite believers in Christ.

Verse 14:

"For the body is not one member but many."

Paul reiterates the diversity of members within the body, emphasizing that it is composed of many different parts. This diversity is essential for the body's proper functioning.

Verse 15:

"If the foot shall say, Because I am not the hand, I am not of the body; is it, therefore, not of the body?"

Paul uses a hypothetical example of the foot and the hand to illustrate that each part of the body has its distinct function. No part should consider itself less important because of its unique role; every part is essential for the body's completeness.

Verse 16:

"And if the ear shall say, Because I am not the eye, I am not of the body; is it, therefore, not of the body?"

Paul continues with another example, contrasting the ear and the eye. Just as the foot and the hand have different functions, so do the ear and the eye. However, the ear should not devalue its role within the body of Christ.

Verse 17:

"If the whole body were an eye, where were the hearing? If the whole were hearing, where were the smelling?"

Paul uses hyperbolic language to emphasize the need for diversity in the body. If the entire body were one part, it would lack the functions of the other parts. The diversity of gifts and roles is essential for the body's overall functioning.

Verse 18:

"But now hath God set the members, every one of them, in the body, as it hath pleased him."

Paul reminds the Corinthians that God is the one who has placed each member, with their unique gifts and roles, within the body. This arrangement is according to God's sovereign pleasure and purpose.

Verse 19:

"And if they were all one member, where were the body?"

Paul reiterates that if all believers were the same, with the same gifts and roles, there would be no complete body. The existence of a diverse body with various functions is necessary for its health and effectiveness.

Verse 20:

"But now are they many members yet but one body."

Paul concludes by emphasizing the present reality: there are many diverse members, but they together form one unified body. The diversity within the body of Christ is not a weakness but a strength, as it allows for a wide range of functions and contributions to the church's mission.

In 1 Corinthians 12:11-20, Paul emphasizes the unity and diversity within the body of Christ. He highlights that the Holy Spirit is the source of all spiritual gifts, and it is the Spirit who sovereignly distributes these gifts to believers. The analogy of the body illustrates the importance of diversity within the church, with each member playing a unique and essential role. Believers are unified in Christ, and their various gifts and functions contribute to the overall health and effectiveness of the body of Christ.

Verse 21:

"And the eye cannot say unto the hand, I have no need of thee: nor again the head to the feet, I have no need of you."

Paul continues his analogy of the body, emphasizing the interdependence of its various parts. Just as the eye cannot dismiss the importance of the hand, or the head cannot disregard the feet, no member of the body of Christ should consider itself unnecessary or unimportant. All have a role to play.

Verse 22:

"Nay, much more those members of the body, which seem to be more feeble, are necessary."

Paul counters any notions of insignificance by highlighting that even those members of the body that might appear weaker or less prominent are still vital. Every part of the body serves a necessary purpose.

Verse 23:

"And those members of the body, which we think to be less honorable, upon these we bestow more abundant honor, and our uncomely parts have more abundant comeliness."

Paul reinforces the idea that members who are considered less honorable or less presentable receive even greater honor and attention. This demonstrates the care and concern that the body should have for all its members, regardless of their outward appearances or perceived importance.

Verse 24:

"For our comely parts have no need: but God hath tempered the body together, having given more abundant honor to that part which lacked."

Paul explains that the more attractive or presentable parts of the body don't require additional attention, whereas God, in His wisdom, has carefully combined and composed the body, ensuring that those parts considered less significant receive greater honor and care. This reflects God's divine ordering and purpose.

Verse 25:

"That there should be no schism in the body, but that the members should have the same care one for another."

Paul's primary concern is the unity of the body. He wants to prevent division or schisms within the church. Instead, he emphasizes that members should care for one another equally, fostering a sense of mutual support and interconnectedness.

Verse 26:

"And whether one member suffer, all the members suffer with it; or one member be honored, all the members rejoice with it."

Paul underscores the idea of unity and empathy within the body. When one member experiences suffering or honor, the entire body should share in the experience. This emphasizes the interconnectedness and mutual concern among believers.

Verse 27:

"Now ye are the body of Christ, and members in particular."

Paul explicitly states that the Corinthian believers collectively make up the body of Christ, with each individual being a member of this body. This reinforces the importance of recognizing their unity and diversity within the church.

Verse 28:

"And God hath set some in the church, first apostles, secondarily prophets, thirdly teachers, after that, miracles, then gifts of healings, helps, governments, diversities of tongues."

Paul lists various roles and gifts within the church, illustrating the diversity of functions and responsibilities. This list includes apostles, prophets, teachers, those with the gift of miracles, those with gifts of healing, helpers, administrators, and those with different kinds of languages (tongues). These roles and gifts contribute to the body's overall effectiveness and ministry.

Verse 29:

"Are all apostles? Are all prophets? Are all teachers? Are all workers of miracles?"

Paul's questions emphasize that not everyone has the same role or gift within the body of Christ. He highlights the diversity of gifts and functions, emphasizing that not all are identical or serve the same purpose.

Verse 30:

"Have all the gifts of healing? Do all speak with tongues? Do all interpret?"

Paul continues to emphasize the diversity of gifts and their distribution. He questions whether everyone possesses gifts like healing, speaking in tongues, or interpreting tongues. The answer is implied as "no," highlighting the uniqueness of individual gifts.

Verse 31:

"But covet earnestly the best gifts: and yet show I unto you a more excellent way."

Paul encourages believers to desire or covet the best gifts earnestly. However, he hints at a "more excellent way" that he will explain in the following chapter, which leads into his famous discourse on love in 1 Corinthians 13.

In 1 Corinthians 12:21-31, Paul continues his analogy of the body to emphasize the interdependence of members within the body of Christ. He stresses that every member, regardless of their perceived significance, is vital for the body's health and unity. Paul encourages mutual care and empathy within the church, underscoring the interconnectedness of believers. He lists various roles and gifts within the church, highlighting their diversity and the fact that not all members have the same function or gift. Finally, he encourages believers to earnestly desire the best gifts while foreshadowing a more excellent way, which he will expound upon in the following chapter, focusing on the importance of love in the exercise of spiritual gifts.

CHAPTER 13

The Supremacy of Love

The theme of 1 Corinthians chapter 13 is "The Supremacy of Love." This chapter is often referred to as the "Love Chapter" because it provides a profound and beautiful description of the nature and importance of love within the Christian community. The central theme revolves around the surpassing value of love as the most excellent and essential attribute for believers to possess and practice. Here's an overview of the main themes and points in 1 Corinthians chapter 13:

1. The Priority of Love (1 Corinthians 13:1-3): Paul begins by emphasizing that without love, even the most remarkable spiritual gifts,

eloquence, and sacrificial acts are meaningless. Love is the foundational quality that gives purpose and significance to all other actions.

2. The Characteristics of Love (1 Corinthians 13:4-7) Paul provides a detailed description of love, highlighting its attributes and behaviors. Love is patient, kind, not envious, not boastful, not proud, not self-seeking, not easily angered, and keeps no record of wrongs. It rejoices in truth and protects, trusts, hopes, and perseveres.

3. The Permanence of Love (1 Corinthians 13:8-13): Paul contrasts the temporary nature of spiritual gifts with the enduring nature of love. Love will never fail or cease to exist. He asserts that faith, hope, and love are essential, but love is the greatest. In the end, knowledge and prophecy will pass away, but love remains.

The central theme of 1 Corinthians chapter 13 is the extraordinary value and indispensability of love in the life of a believer and within the Christian community. Paul underscores that love is the foundation upon which all other virtues and actions should be built. The chapter encourages believers to strive for and practice love in all aspects of their lives, reflecting the love that God has for us.

Verse 1:

"Though I speak with the tongues of men and of angels and have not charity, I am become as sounding brass, or a tinkling cymbal."

Paul begins by emphasizing the paramount importance of love (charity). He acknowledges the value of eloquent speech, even the ability to speak in human and angelic languages, but underscores that without love, such speech is empty and devoid of meaning. It's like noise, akin to the clanging of brass or cymbals.

Verse 2:

"And though I have the gift of prophecy and understand all mysteries and all knowledge, and though I have all faith, so that I could remove mountains, and have not charity, I am nothing."

Paul extends the importance of love to spiritual gifts and understanding. Even possessing the gift of prophecy, deep knowledge, and unwavering faith, without love, renders an individual insignificant. Love is the vital ingredient that gives purpose and value to these gifts and qualities.

Verse 3:

"And though I bestow all my goods to feed the poor, and though I give my body to be burned and have not charity, it profiteth me nothing."

Paul continues to emphasize the significance of love by mentioning acts of selflessness, such as giving away one's possessions to help the poor or even sacrificing one's life for a noble cause. Without love, such acts hold no inherent value. Love is the driving force behind genuine self-sacrifice and generosity.

Verse 4:

"Charity suffereth long, and is kind; charity envieth not; charity vaunteth not itself, is not puffed up,"

Paul begins to describe the nature of love. Love is characterized by patience and kindness. It does not envy or boast; it is not proud or arrogant.

Verse 5:

"Doth not behave itself unseemly, seeketh not her own, is not easily provoked, thinketh no evil;"

Love is considerate of others and does not act inappropriately or selfishly. It is not quick to anger and doesn't keep a record of wrongs or harbor ill thoughts toward others.

Verse 6:

"Rejoiceth not in iniquity but rejoiceth in the truth;"

Love does not find joy in wrongdoing or injustice but takes delight in the truth, righteousness, and goodness.

Verse 7:

"Beareth all things, believeth all things, hopeth all things, endureth all things."

Love is characterized by endurance and resilience. It can bear the weight of difficult circumstances, maintain faith, hold on to hope, and persevere through adversity.

Verse 8:

"Charity never faileth, but whether there be prophecies, they shall fail; whether there be tongues, they shall cease; whether there be knowledge, it shall vanish away."

Paul emphasizes the enduring nature of love. Love never fails or ceases to be relevant. He contrasts love with spiritual gifts like prophecy, speaking in tongues, and knowledge, all of which are temporal and will eventually come to an end.

Verse 9:

"For we know in part and we prophesy in part."

Paul acknowledges the limited and partial nature of human knowledge and prophetic insight. Even the most profound human

wisdom and spiritual understanding are incomplete in comparison to God's perfect knowledge.
Verse 10:

"But when that which is perfect is come, then that which is in part shall be done away."

Paul anticipates a future state where the partial knowledge and prophecies will give way to something perfect. This perfection is often understood as the consummation of God's Kingdom or the return of Christ, where human understanding will be completed and no longer partial.

In 1 Corinthians 13:1-10, Paul eloquently expounds on the central theme of love. He highlights that love is of paramount importance, even surpassing the value of spiritual gifts, knowledge, and self-sacrifice. Love is characterized by patience, kindness, humility, and a focus on the well-being of others. It stands in stark contrast to arrogance, envy, and selfishness. Paul affirms that love never fails, enduring through all circumstances, while spiritual gifts and knowledge are limited and temporary. This chapter underscores the enduring and foundational role of love in the life of a Christian and in the community of believers.
Verse 11:

"When I was a child, I spake as a child, I understood as a child, I thought as a child: but when I became a man, I put away childish things."

Paul uses a metaphor to illustrate the growth and maturity of the believer. In the context of spiritual development, he compares the understanding and perspective of a child to that of an adult. He emphasizes the idea that as Christians mature in faith, they should leave behind immature, self-centered ways of thinking and acting.
Verse 12:

"For now, we see through a glass, darkly, but then face to face: now I know in part, but then shall I know even as also I am known."

Paul explains that in the present, human understanding of spiritual matters is limited and somewhat obscure, like looking at a reflection in a dimly lit mirror. However, in the future, when believers are in the presence of God, their understanding will be complete and clear, and they will fully comprehend even as they themselves are fully known by God.

Verse 13:

"And now abideth faith, hope, charity, these three; but the greatest of these is charity."

Paul concludes by highlighting three enduring virtues: faith, hope, and charity (love). While faith and hope are vital aspects of the Christian walk, he emphasizes that love (charity) surpasses them all in importance. Love is the greatest because it is central to the Christian life, relationships, and the character of God.

In 1 Corinthians 13:11-13, Paul uses the metaphor of childhood to adulthood to illustrate the concept of spiritual growth and maturity. He emphasizes that spiritual understanding in the present is partial and somewhat obscure but that one day believers will have complete knowledge in the presence of God. He then identifies three enduring virtues: faith, hope, and love. While faith and hope are significant, love holds the highest place, serving as the foundation for the Christian life and relationships. This chapter concludes with an affirmation of love's supreme importance in the life of a believer.

Orderly Worship and the Gifts of the Spirit

The theme of 1 Corinthians chapter 14 is "Orderly Worship and the Gifts of the Spirit." In this chapter, the Apostle Paul addresses the use of spiritual gifts, particularly the gift of speaking in tongues and prophecy, within the context of the worship assembly. The central theme revolves around the importance of maintaining order and edification in the church's gatherings. Here's an overview of the main themes and points in 1 Corinthians chapter 14:

1. The Value of Prophecy Over Tongues (1 Corinthians 14:1-5): Paul emphasizes the superiority of prophecy over speaking in tongues within the corporate worship setting. He explains that prophecy is more beneficial for the edification of the church, while speaking in tongues is primarily a personal communication with God.

2. The Need for Clarity in Worship (1 Corinthians 14:6-19): Paul underscores the importance of clear and understandable communication during worship. He mentions that speaking in tongues without interpretation can be confusing for the congregation and is less edifying. He encourages believers to prioritize the edification of others.

3. Regulating Tongues in the Assembly (1 Corinthians 14:20-33): Paul provides guidelines for the proper use of tongues in the worship assembly. He suggests that if tongues are spoken, there should be interpretation, or else it should be done privately between the individual and God. Paul also emphasizes the principle of orderly worship, with each member contributing to the edification of the whole.

4. The Role of Women in Worship (1 Corinthians 14:34-40): Paul briefly addresses the role of women in the worship assembly, emphasizing that they should not disrupt the meeting but should learn quietly. His primary concern is the maintenance of order and decency in worship.

The central theme in 1 Corinthians chapter 14 is the need for order, clarity, and edification in the corporate worship of the church. Paul encourages believers to use their spiritual gifts, especially in prophecy and speaking in tongues, in a way that benefits the entire congregation and promotes understanding. The chapter serves as a guide for conducting worship services that are spiritually enriching and edifying to all participants.

Verse 1:

"Follow after charity, and desire spiritual gifts, but rather that ye may prophesy."

Paul begins this chapter by encouraging the Corinthians to prioritize love (charity) and the pursuit of spiritual gifts. He specifically highlights the value of the gift of prophecy, which involves speaking God's messages to others for edification, encouragement, and comfort.

Verse 2:

"For he that speaketh in an unknown tongue speaketh not unto men, but unto God: for no man understandeth him; howbeit in the spirit he speaketh mysteries."

Paul contrasts speaking in tongues (languages unknown to the speaker and the listeners) with prophesying. Speaking in tongues, while a genuine spiritual gift, primarily involves communication between the speaker and God, as it is often an unknown language. Although it may involve deep spiritual experiences, it doesn't convey a clear message to the assembly.

Verse 3:

"But he that prophesieth speaketh unto men to edification, and exhortation, and comfort."

In contrast to speaking in tongues, prophesying directly benefits the church. The message is intended for the understanding and edification of the believers. It serves to build up, encourage, and bring comfort to the community.

Verse 4:

"He that speaketh in an unknown tongue edifieth himself, but he that prophesieth edifieth the church."

Paul underscores the contrast: speaking in tongues primarily benefits the individual who speaks, fostering personal spiritual growth.

In contrast, prophesying benefits the entire church community by providing clear and understandable messages that encourage and build up others.

Verse 5:

"I would that ye all spake with tongues but rather that ye prophesied: for greater is he that prophesieth than he that speaketh with tongues, except he interprets, that the church may receive edifying."

Paul expresses a desire for the Corinthians to possess the gift of speaking in tongues, but he emphasizes the superiority of prophesying. However, if someone speaks in tongues, an interpretation is needed for the message to edify the church, further highlighting the value of clear communication within the assembly.

Verse 6:

"Now, brethren, if I come unto you speaking with tongues, what shall I profit you, except I shall speak to you either by revelation, or by knowledge, or by prophesying, or by doctrine?"

Paul emphasizes the importance of meaningful and intelligible communication. When he visits the Corinthians, speaking in tongues alone won't be profitable to them. Instead, he intends to provide revelation, knowledge, prophecy, or doctrine—messages that can be understood and benefit the congregation.

Verse 7:

"And even things without life giving sound, whether pipe or harp, except they give a distinction in the sounds, how shall it be known what is piped or harped?"

Paul uses a simple illustration to highlight the need for distinct and recognizable sounds. Just as a musical instrument must produce distinct notes to create a melody, clear communication is essential for understanding the message.

Verse 8:

"For if the trumpet gives an uncertain sound, who shall prepare himself to the battle?"

Paul extends the metaphor by referencing the use of a trumpet in military contexts. A trumpet's call must be clear and distinct, as it signals important actions in battle. Unclear signals would lead to confusion and ineffective preparation.

Verse 9:

"So likewise, ye, except ye utter by the tongue words easy to be understood, how shall it be known what is spoken? For ye shall speak into the air."

Paul returns to the Corinthians, emphasizing the necessity of speaking words that are easy to understand. Otherwise, the speaker is essentially talking to the air, as the message isn't benefiting anyone due to lack of comprehension.

Verse 10:

"There are, it may be, so many kinds of voices in the world, and none of them is without significance."

Paul acknowledges the diversity of languages and voices in the world. He emphasizes that each voice carries meaning and significance. Therefore, clarity and understanding in communication are essential, especially within the context of the church.

In 1 Corinthians 14:1-10, Paul addresses the use of spiritual gifts, particularly speaking in tongues and prophesying, within the church. He emphasizes the value of prophecy, which provides clear and understandable messages for the edification of the church. Paul stresses the importance of intelligible communication, drawing analogies to music and military signals. He encourages the Corinthians to prioritize speaking words that are easy to understand to ensure that the message has significance and benefits the church. Clarity and understanding in communication are essential in the context of worship and teaching within the Christian community.

Verse 11:

"Therefore, if I know not the meaning of the voice, I shall be unto him that speaketh a barbarian, and he that speaketh shall be a barbarian unto me."

Paul continues to stress the importance of comprehensible communication. If a person cannot understand the language or message being spoken, both the speaker and the listener become like "barbarians" to each other, unable to connect or convey meaning.

Verse 12:

"Even so ye, forasmuch as ye are zealous of spiritual gifts, seek that ye may excel to the edifying of the church."

Paul acknowledges the Corinthians' zeal for spiritual gifts but directs them to prioritize gifts that promote the edification (building up) of the church. Spiritual gifts should serve the communal good rather than personal spiritual experiences.

Verse 13:

"Wherefore let him that speaketh in an unknown tongue pray that he may interpret."

Paul advises those who speak in tongues to pray for the gift of interpretation. This emphasizes the need for clarity and understanding when using the gift of speaking in tongues in a corporate setting.

Verse 14:

"For if I pray in an unknown tongue, my spirit prayeth, but my understanding is unfruitful."

Paul contrasts praying in tongues with praying with understanding. Praying in tongues may be a valid spiritual experience, but it doesn't engage the understanding. He encourages prayer with both spirit and understanding to be fruitful and edifying.

Verse 15:

"What is it then? I will pray with the spirit, and I will pray with the understanding also: I will sing with the spirit, and I will sing with the understanding also."

Paul articulates his intent: he will pray and sing both with the spirit (in tongues or under the influence of the Holy Spirit) and with understanding. He values a balance that includes the personal spiritual experience and the ability to convey meaning to others.

Verse 16:

"Else when thou shalt bless with the spirit, how shall he that occupieth the room of the unlearned say Amen at thy giving of thanks, seeing he understandeth not what thou sayest?"

Paul underscores the practical challenge of edifying others. If someone blesses or gives thanks in tongues, how can an unlearned person present say "Amen" if they don't understand the blessing? "Amen" is an affirmation of agreement, which necessitates comprehension.

Verse 17:

"For thou verily givest thanks well, but the other is not edified."

Paul acknowledges that speaking in tongues can be a genuine expression of thanks and praise to God. However, if others present don't understand it, they are not edified or built up by it. The goal is to benefit the whole assembly.

Verse 18:

"I thank my God I speak with tongues more than ye all."

Paul indicates that he is not opposed to speaking in tongues; in fact, he personally values it. He thanks God for the gift of speaking in tongues but emphasizes the importance of balance and edification in the church.

Verse 19:

"Yet in the church I had rather speak five words with my understanding, that by my voice I might teach others also, than ten thousand words in an unknown tongue."

Paul's emphasis on understanding and teaching is clear. He values speaking five intelligible words that can teach and edify others more than speaking ten thousand words in an unknown tongue, which lack understanding and edification.

Verse 20:

"Brethren, be not children in understanding: howbeit in malice be ye children, but in understanding be men."

Paul encourages the Corinthians to be mature in their understanding, not like children. In matters of malice (harmful intentions), they should be innocent like children, but when it comes to understanding, they should act maturely, thinking and speaking in ways that edify and teach.

In 1 Corinthians 14:11-20, Paul continues to address the use of spiritual gifts, particularly the gift of speaking in tongues, within the context of the church. He stresses the importance of understanding and edification, encouraging believers to pray and sing with both their spirits and their understanding. Paul values speaking in tongues but highlights the need for balance, clarity, and the edification of the entire congregation. His goal is to promote teaching, comprehension, and the spiritual growth of the church members.

Verse 21:

"In the law it is written, with men of other tongues and other lips will I speak unto this people, and yet for all that will they not hear me, saith the Lord."

Paul references a prophecy from the Old Testament, specifically from the book of Isaiah (Isaiah 28:11-12). The prophecy speaks of God's intention to communicate with people through foreign languages and messages, indicating a form of judgment and a call for repentance. In the context of Paul's argument, he highlights that speaking in tongues might resemble this prophecy but emphasizes that the Corinthians should still strive for understanding and edification when using the gift.

Verse 22:

"Wherefore tongues are for a sign, not to them that believe, but to them that believe not: but prophesying serveth not for them that believe not but for them which believe."

Paul distinguishes the roles of speaking in tongues and prophesying. Tongues serve as a sign primarily to unbelievers, as they may perceive it as supernatural and be prompted to consider the message being conveyed. On the other hand, prophecy is more beneficial to believers, as it provides direct understanding and edification.

Verse 23:

"If, therefore, the whole church be come together into one place, and all speak with tongues, and there come in those that are unlearned, or unbelievers, will they not say that ye are mad?"

Paul addresses a practical concern. If everyone in the church speaks in tongues when outsiders, particularly unlearned or unbelieving individuals, visit, they might perceive the congregation as chaotic or even "mad" because they won't understand the messages being conveyed.

Verse 24:

"But if all prophesy, and there come in one that believeth not, or one unlearned, he is convinced of all, he is judged of all:"

In contrast, if everyone prophesies, and an unbeliever or unlearned person visits, they can be convinced and judged by the message, as it is comprehensible and intended for their understanding. Prophecy can lead to conviction and understanding.

Verse 25:

"And thus are the secrets of his heart made manifest, and so, falling down on his face, he will worship God, and report that God is in you of a truth."

Paul explains the potential impact of prophesying on an unbeliever or unlearned individual. Through prophesy, the person's inner thoughts and secrets can be revealed, leading to a deep conviction and response. They may worship God and acknowledge that God's presence is truly among the believers.

Verse 26:

"How is it then, brethren? when ye come together, every one of you hath a psalm, hath a doctrine, hath a tongue, hath a revelation, hath an interpretation. Let all things be done unto edifying."

Paul addresses the issue of disorderly gatherings. He notes that many individuals in the Corinthian church come with various spiritual gifts and expressions, such as psalms, doctrines, tongues, revelations, and interpretations. However, he emphasizes that everything should be done for the purpose of edification—building up the body of believers.

Verse 27:

"If any man speak in an unknown tongue, let it be by two, or at the most by three, and that by course, and let one interpret."

Paul introduces guidelines for speaking in tongues during gatherings. He suggests that only two or at most three individuals should speak in tongues, and they should take turns. Moreover, there should be an interpreter present to ensure that the message can be understood and edify the church.

Verse 28:

"But if there be no interpreter, let him keep silence in the church, and let him speak to himself and to God."

Paul emphasizes the importance of interpretation. If no one is present to interpret the message, those with the gift of speaking in tongues should remain silent in the church and speak to God privately. This maintains order and prioritizes understanding.

Verse 29:

"Let the prophets speak two or three, and let the other judge."

Paul also provides guidelines for prophesying. He suggests that two or three individuals should speak, while others should act as judges, discerning the message's alignment with God's truth and edification.

Verse 30:

"If anything, be revealed to another that sitteth by, let the first hold his peace."

Paul encourages an orderly and respectful approach to prophecy. If someone receives a revelation while another is speaking, the first person should wait for their turn rather than interrupt the current speaker.

In 1 Corinthians 14:21-30, Paul discusses the roles of speaking in tongues and prophesying within the church. He references an Old Testament prophecy and highlights that speaking in tongues can be a sign for unbelievers. He stresses the importance of order and understanding in gatherings, especially when outsiders are present. Paul encourages speaking in tongues with interpretation, emphasizing the edification of the church. He provides guidelines for the use of both gifts, ensuring that everything is done in an orderly and edifying manner for the benefit of all present.

Verse 31:

"For ye may all prophesy one by one, that all may learn, and all may be comforted."

Paul encourages orderly and edifying prophecy within the congregation. He suggests that all believers can take turns prophesying, one by one. This practice allows everyone to learn from the messages and find comfort in them.

Verse 32:

"And the spirits of the prophets are subject to the prophets."

Paul emphasizes that those with the gift of prophecy can control their expression of it. This means that they can choose when and how to use their spiritual gift within the bounds of order and edification.

Verse 33:

"For God is not the author of confusion, but of peace, as in all churches of the saints."

Paul underscores the principle of order within the church. He states that God is not a God of confusion but of peace. This order and peace should be characteristic of all Christian gatherings in various churches.

Verse 34:

"Let your women keep silence in the churches, for it is not permitted unto them to speak, but they are commanded to be under obedience, as also saith the law."

This verse has been a source of debate and interpretation. Some understand it to suggest that women should remain silent in church and not speak or hold leadership roles. However, it's important to consider the broader context and other passages in the New Testament that show women playing active roles in the early church. Interpretations vary, and some believe this may have been addressing specific disruptive behavior in the Corinthian church.

Verse 35:

"And if they will learn anything, let them ask their husbands at home, for it is a shame for women to speak in the church."

This verse seems to continue the instruction about women's behavior in the church. It suggests that if women have questions or desire to learn, they should ask their husbands at home rather than disrupt the church service with their inquiries. Again, it's essential to consider the cultural and historical context of this passage.

Verse 36:

"What? came the word of God out from you? or came it unto you only?"

Paul uses a rhetorical question to challenge the Corinthians. He implies that the Corinthians are not the sole possessors or originators of God's Word. The Word of God is not exclusive to them, but it is a universal message that applies to all believers and churches.

Verse 37:

"If any man think himself to be a prophet or spiritual, let him acknowledge that the things that I write unto you are the commandments of the Lord."

Paul reaffirms the authority of his teachings and writings as being rooted in the commandments of the Lord. He calls on those who consider themselves prophets or spiritual to acknowledge the divine authority of his instructions.

Verse 38:

"But if any man be ignorant, let him be ignorant."

Paul acknowledges that not everyone will accept his teaching, and if someone chooses to remain ignorant or disobedient to these commandments, they will have to bear the consequences of their choice.

Verse 39:

"Wherefore, brethren, covet to prophesy and forbid not to speak with tongues."

Paul reiterates the importance of desiring the gift of prophecy and encourages speaking in tongues, as long as it is done decently and in order. He emphasizes the balance between spiritual gifts and the need for proper conduct.

Verse 40:

"Let all things be done decently and in order."

Paul's final instruction serves as a summary and overarching principle. Everything in the church, whether it involves spiritual gifts, speech, or conduct, should be characterized by decency and orderliness, ensuring that the gathering is edifying and peaceful.

In 1 Corinthians 14:31-40, Paul continues to provide guidance on the use of spiritual gifts, specifically prophecy and speaking in tongues. He emphasizes the importance of orderly and edifying prophecy, the control that prophets have over their gift, and the principle that God is a God of order and peace. The passage addressing women's conduct in the church has generated various interpretations and should be understood in its cultural and historical context. Paul reaffirms the authority of his teachings and underscores the importance of conducting all aspects of church life decently and in an orderly manner, ensuring that everything is done for the benefit of the congregation.

∾

CHAPTER 15

The Resurrection of the Dead

The theme of 1 Corinthians chapter 15 is "The Resurrection of the Dead." In this chapter, the Apostle Paul addresses the doctrine of the resurrection of the dead, emphasizing the central role of the resurrection in the Christian faith. The chapter discusses the resurrection of Christ and its implications for believers, as well as the nature of the resurrection body. Here's an overview of the main themes and points in 1 Corinthians chapter 15:

1. The Gospel of the Resurrection (1 Corinthians 15:1-11): Paul begins by reminding the Corinthians of the gospel he preached to them, which includes the resurrection of Christ. He highlights the foundational nature of the resurrection in the Christian message.

2. The Importance of Christ's Resurrection (1 Corinthians 15:12-19): Paul argues that if there is no resurrection of the dead, including Christ's resurrection, then faith in Christ is in vain, and believers are still in their sins. He emphasizes the centrality of Christ's resurrection to the Christian faith.

3. The Order of Resurrection (1 Corinthians 15:20-28): Paul explains the order of resurrection, with Christ being the firstfruits of the dead. He describes a future event in which all things will be subjected to Christ, and death will be finally defeated.

4. The Nature of the Resurrection Body (1 Corinthians 15:35-49): Paul addresses questions about the nature of the resurrection body. He compares the natural body to the spiritual body, explaining that the resurrection body will be imperishable, glorious, and transformed.

5. The Victory Over Death (1 Corinthians 15:50-58): Paul concludes by emphasizing the victory over death through the resurrection of believers. He speaks of the transformation that will occur at the last trumpet and the victorious nature of faith in Christ.

The central theme in 1 Corinthians chapter 15 is the resurrection of the dead, especially the resurrection of Christ and the future resurrection of believers. Paul underscores the essential role of the resurrection in the Christian faith, affirming its reality and the hope it brings to all who believe. The chapter serves to strengthen the Corinthians' understanding of this fundamental doctrine and its implications for their lives.

Verse 1:

"Moreover, brethren, I declare unto you the gospel which I preached unto you, which also ye have received, and wherein ye stand;"

Paul begins this chapter by addressing the Corinthians as "brethren" and stating his intention to declare the gospel he previously preached to them. He emphasizes that the Corinthians have received and accepted this gospel, and it is the foundation upon which they stand.

Verse 2:

"By which also ye are saved if ye keep in memory what I preached unto you unless ye have believed in vain."

Paul highlights the importance of continuing to believe and remember the gospel message they received. Salvation is contingent on a genuine and enduring faith, and he warns against a belief that proves to be in vain or insincere.

Verse 3:

"For I delivered unto you first of all that which I also received, how that Christ died for our sins according to the scriptures;"

Paul reiterates the core message of the gospel that he received and passed on to the Corinthians. He emphasizes the fulfillment of Old Testament prophecies, indicating that Christ's death was for the purpose of atoning for our sins.

Verse 4:

"And that he was buried, and that he rose again the third day according to the scriptures:"

Paul continues to explain key elements of the gospel message: Christ's burial and resurrection. He emphasizes the resurrection as being in line with the scriptures, affirming the prophetic nature of these events.

Verse 5:

"And that he was seen of Cephas, then of the twelve:"

Paul provides evidence for the resurrection by listing witnesses. Cephas (Peter) and the twelve apostles were among the first to see the risen Christ, corroborating the truth of His resurrection.

Verse 6:

"After that, he was seen of above five hundred brethren at once, of whom the greater part remains unto this present, but some are fallen asleep."

Paul mentions a significant event in which Christ was seen by over 500 believers simultaneously. Many of these witnesses were still alive at the time of Paul's writing, offering further proof of the resurrection.

Verse 7:

"After that, he was seen of James, then of all the apostles."

Paul continues to list witnesses of the resurrected Christ, including James (likely referring to James, the half-brother of Jesus) and all the apostles. These appearances provided undeniable evidence of Christ's resurrection.

Verse 8:

"And last of all he was seen of me also, as of one born out of due time."

Paul humbly includes himself as a witness to the risen Christ. He describes his own experience of encountering Jesus on the road to Damascus as being like one "born out of due time," suggesting his unexpected and unique apostleship.

Verse 9:

"For I am the least of the apostles, that am not meet to be called an apostle because I persecuted the church of God."

Paul acknowledges his unworthiness to be called an apostle, especially given his history of persecuting the early Christian community. Despite his past, he was chosen by God and appointed as an apostle.

Verse 10:

"But by the grace of God I am what I am, and his grace which was bestowed upon me was not in vain, but I labored more abundantly than they all, yet not I, but the grace of God which was with me."

Paul attributes his apostleship and his accomplishments in spreading the gospel to the grace of God. He recognizes that it was not in vain and that he worked diligently, but he also emphasizes that it was the grace of God that empowered and guided his efforts.

In 1 Corinthians 15:1-10, Paul delivers a powerful exposition of the gospel message. He emphasizes the core elements of the gospel: Christ's death for our sins, His burial, and His resurrection, all in accordance with the Scriptures. Paul provides a list of witnesses to the resurrected Christ, including himself. He acknowledges his past as a persecutor of the church but attributes his transformation and apostleship to the grace of God. This passage serves as a strong affirmation of the resurrection and the foundational importance of the gospel in the life of a believer and the church.

Verse 11:

"Therefore, whether it was I or they, so we preach, and so ye believed."

Paul underscores the unity in preaching the gospel message. Whether he or other apostles preached, the content of the gospel remained consistent. The Corinthians' faith was rooted in the message they received from the apostles.

Verse 12:

"Now if Christ be preached that he rose from the dead, how say some among you that there is no resurrection of the dead?"

Paul addresses a perplexing issue in the Corinthian church. While the gospel they received proclaims the resurrection of Christ, some members of the congregation are denying the general resurrection of the dead. This contradiction within their beliefs creates a theological inconsistency.

Verse 13:

"But if there be no resurrection of the dead, then is Christ not risen."

Paul presents the logical consequence of denying the resurrection of the dead. If there is no general resurrection, then Christ, who is at the heart of the Christian message, could not have been raised from the dead.

Verse 14:

"And if Christ be not risen, then is our preaching vain, and your faith is also vain."

Paul underscores the centrality of the resurrection in Christian faith. If Christ has not been raised from the dead, the entire foundation of their faith and the preaching of the gospel become empty and meaningless.

Verse 15:

"Yea, and we are found false witnesses of God because we have testified of God that he raised up Christ, whom he raised not up, if so be that the dead rise not."

Paul acknowledges the serious implications of preaching a false resurrection. If Christ has not been raised, the apostles are essentially false witnesses testifying to something that did not occur, which would be a grave offense.

Verse 16:

"For if the dead rise not, then is not Christ raised."

Paul reiterates the inseparable connection between the general resurrection and Christ's resurrection. If the dead do not rise, then Christ could not have been raised.

Verse 17:

"And if Christ be not raised, your faith is vain; ye are yet in your sins."

Paul emphasizes the consequences of Christ not being raised. In such a scenario, their faith is futile, and they remain in their sins without the hope of redemption through Christ's atoning work.

Verse 18:

"Then they also which are fallen asleep in Christ are perished."

Paul extends the ramifications of Christ not being raised to those who have died as believers. If there is no resurrection, even those who have died in faith have no hope of eternal life.

Verse 19:

"If in this life only we have hope in Christ, we are of all men most miserable."

Paul highlights the futility of faith in Christ if it is limited to this earthly life only. If there is no resurrection and no hope of eternal life, the Christian experience is one of misery, as it lacks the promise of ultimate redemption.

Verse 20:

"But now is Christ risen from the dead and become the firstfruits of them that slept."

Paul brings the focus back to the resurrection of Christ as a present reality. He declares with certainty that Christ has indeed been raised from the dead, becoming the "firstfruits" or the first in a harvest of those who have died. This resurrection of Christ is the foundation of the Christian hope for the future.

In 1 Corinthians 15:11-20, Paul addresses the issue of resurrection within the Corinthian church. He underscores the essential connection between the resurrection of Christ and the hope of the general resurrection of the dead. If there is no resurrection, the entire Christian faith is in vain, and believers have no hope beyond this life. However, Paul affirms the reality of Christ's resurrection, which serves as the firstfruits of the future resurrection of all believers. The resurrection of Christ is the cornerstone of the Christian faith, providing hope for eternal life and the redemption of those who have died in faith.

Verse 21:

"For since by man came death, by man came also the resurrection of the dead."

Paul highlights the role of humanity in both death and resurrection. Death came through Adam's sin, but resurrection from the dead comes through the redemptive work of Jesus Christ, often referred to as the "second Adam."

Verse 22:

"For as in Adam all die, even so in Christ shall all be made alive."

Paul draws a parallel between Adam's role in humanity's fall and Christ's role in humanity's restoration. Just as all inherit mortality through Adam, all can experience resurrection and eternal life through their connection to Christ.

Verse 23:

"But every man in his own order: Christ the firstfruits; afterward they that are Christ's at his coming."

Paul explains the order of resurrection. Christ is the firstfruits, being the first to rise from the dead to eternal life. Following Him, all believers who are "in Christ" will experience resurrection at His return.

Verse 24:

"Then cometh the end when he shall have delivered up the kingdom to God, even the Father, when he shall have put down all rule and all authority and power."

Paul speaks of a future event when Christ will hand over His kingdom to God the Father. At that time, all opposing rule, authority, and power will be nullified, and God's supreme authority will be established.

Verse 25:

"For he must reign until he hath put all enemies under his feet."

Paul emphasizes that Christ's reign will continue until all opposition and enemies are subdued under His authority.

Verse 26:

"The last enemy that shall be destroyed is death."

Paul identifies death as the final enemy to be conquered. In the ultimate consummation of God's plan, death itself will be defeated, and believers will be raised to eternal life.

Verse 27:

"For he hath put all things under his feet. But when he saith all things are put under him, it is manifest that he is excepted, which did put all things under him."

Paul recognizes that God the Father has subjected all things under the authority of Christ. However, it's important to understand that the Father Himself is not subject to Christ but remains sovereign over all.

Verse 28:

"And when all things shall be subdued unto him, then shall the Son also himself be subject unto him that put all things under him, that God may be all in all."

In the final consummation, when all opposition is conquered, Christ will subject Himself to God the Father, and God will be exalted as supreme over all. This points to the ultimate unity of God's purpose and the fulfillment of His plan.

Verse 29:

"Else what shall they do which are baptized for the dead, if the dead rise not at all? why are they then baptized for the dead?"

Paul refers to a practice among some Christians in Corinth who were being baptized on behalf of deceased believers. While this practice remains somewhat enigmatic and debated, Paul uses it to emphasize the importance of the resurrection. Baptism on behalf of the dead would make no sense if there were no hope of resurrection.

Verse 30:

"And why stand we in jeopardy every hour?"

Paul underscores the personal sacrifices and dangers he and other apostles face daily for the sake of preaching the gospel. Their dedication and willingness to endure hardship are driven by their belief in the resurrection and the eternal hope it provides.

In 1 Corinthians 15:21-30, Paul discusses the relationship between Adam's role in humanity's fall and Christ's role in humanity's redemption. He outlines the order of resurrection, the defeat of death as the final enemy, and the ultimate submission of all things to God's authority. Paul also refers to the practice of baptism on behalf of the dead to emphasize the importance of the resurrection. His own sacrifices and those of other apostles are driven by their deep conviction in the hope of resurrection and the truth of the gospel.

Verse 31:

"I protest by your rejoicing which I have in Christ Jesus our Lord, I die daily."

Paul uses strong language to emphasize the intensity of his daily commitment to the gospel. He "dies daily" not in a literal sense but metaphorically, indicating that he faces constant hardships, dangers, and personal sacrifices for the sake of the gospel.

Verse 32:

"If after the manner of men, I have fought with beasts at Ephesus, what advantageth it me if the dead rise not? Let us eat and drink, for tomorrow we die."

Paul refers to a severe and dangerous situation he faced in Ephesus. He contrasts this with the futility of such sacrifices if there is no resurrection. If there's no hope beyond this life, people might as well indulge in self-gratification, but Paul strongly opposes this perspective. Verse 33:

"Be not deceived: evil communications corrupt good manners."

Paul warns against being deceived or influenced by those who deny the resurrection. He emphasizes that associating with those who promote false beliefs can corrupt one's moral conduct. Verse 34:

"Awake to righteousness and sin not, for some have not the knowledge of God. I speak this to your shame."

Paul urges the Corinthians to wake up to righteousness and avoid sin. He points out that some among them lack the knowledge of God, implying that their erroneous beliefs and behaviors bring shame to the community. Verse 35:

"But some man will say, how are the dead raised up? and with what body do they come?"

Paul anticipates questions and objections regarding the resurrection of the dead. Some might wonder about the mechanics of how the dead will be raised and in what form they will come. Verse 36:

"Thou fool, that which thou sowest is not quickened except it die."

Paul uses an analogy from agriculture to explain the concept of resurrection. He compares the process of sowing seeds in the ground, which first die or decompose before new life springs forth. Similarly, the dead are sown, but they will be raised to new life.

Verse 37:

"And that which thou sowest, thou sowest not that body that shall be, but bare grain, it may chance of wheat or of some other grain."

Paul further elaborates on the analogy. When seeds are sown, they do not grow into the same body that was sown but into a new plant. The specific form it takes depends on the type of seed sown.

Verse 38:

"But God giveth it a body as it hath pleased him, and to every seed his own body."

Paul emphasizes that God determines the form and body that each seed will have in the process of growth. Just as in nature, God has the power to grant a new, transformed body to the resurrected dead as He sees fit.

Verse 39:

"All flesh is not the same flesh, but there is one kind of flesh of men, another flesh of beasts, another of fishes, and another of birds."

Paul acknowledges the diversity of flesh in creation. Different creatures have different types of flesh, illustrating the diversity of God's creative work.

Verse 40:

"There are also celestial bodies and bodies terrestrial, but the glory of the celestial is one, and the glory of the terrestrial is another."

Paul draws a distinction between celestial bodies (heavenly bodies) and terrestrial bodies (earthly bodies). Each type has its own unique glory or splendor. This differentiation illustrates the diversity of God's creation in the natural and spiritual realms.

In 1 Corinthians 15:31-40, Paul continues to discuss the concept of the resurrection of the dead. He emphasizes the seriousness of his commitment to the gospel and addresses potential objections and questions about resurrection. Paul uses analogies from agriculture and creation to illustrate the transformation that takes place in the resurrection. He points to the diversity in God's creation, both in the physical and spiritual realms, emphasizing that God determines the nature of the resurrected body.

Verse 41:

"There is one glory of the sun, and another glory of the moon, and another glory of the stars; for one-star differeth from another star in glory."

Paul continues to emphasize the diversity in God's creation. Just as there are different levels of brightness or glory among celestial bodies like the sun, moon, and stars, there will be diversity in the nature and glory of resurrected bodies. The implication is that not all resurrected bodies will be the same.

Verse 42:

"So also, is the resurrection of the dead. It is sown in corruption; it is raised in incorruption."

Paul draws a parallel between the transformation of celestial bodies and the resurrection of the dead. Resurrected bodies, like the stars, will be raised in incorruption, free from decay and imperfection.

Verse 43:

"It is sown in dishonor; it is raised in glory; it is sown in weakness; it is raised in power."

Paul contrasts the condition of the body when it is sown (at death) and when it is raised (in resurrection). Sown in dishonor and weakness, the body is raised in glory and power, signifying a profound transformation.

Verse 44:

"It is sown a natural body; it is raised a spiritual body. There is a natural body, and there is a spiritual body."

Paul makes a clear distinction between the natural body, which is subject to the physical limitations and weaknesses of this world, and the spiritual body, which is free from these constraints and is suited for the spiritual realm.

Verse 45:

"And so, it is written, The first man Adam was made a living soul; the last Adam was made a quickening spirit."

Paul refers to the distinction between the first Adam (referring to the human progenitor, Adam) and the last Adam (referring to Christ). The first Adam was a living soul created from the earth, whereas the last Adam (Christ) is a life-giving spirit who imparts spiritual life.

Verse 46:

"Howbeit that was not first which is spiritual, but that which is natural, and afterward that which is spiritual."

Paul acknowledges the historical sequence—first the natural (Adam) and then the spiritual (Christ). This sequence does not negate the reality of the spiritual realm or the spiritual bodies in the resurrection.

Verse 47:

"The first man is of the earth, earthy; the second man is the Lord from heaven."

Paul emphasizes the origin and nature of the two Adams. The first Adam is earthly and formed from the dust, while the second Adam (Christ) is divine and originates from heaven.

Verse 48:

"As is the earthy, such are they also that are earthy, and as is the heavenly, such are they also that are heavenly."

Paul underscores the connection between the nature of the two Adams and those who are associated with them. Those who are "earthy" (linked to the first Adam) will have natural bodies, while those who are "heavenly" (connected to Christ) will have spiritual bodies.

Verse 49:

"And as we have borne the image of the earthy, we shall also bear the image of the heavenly."

Paul points to the transformation that believers will undergo. Just as they have borne the image of the earthly Adam, they will also bear the image of the heavenly Adam, Christ, in the resurrection.

Verse 50:

"Now this I say, brethren, that flesh and blood cannot inherit the kingdom of God, neither doth corruption inherit incorruption."

Paul reiterates a crucial point: flesh and blood, in their current corruptible state, cannot enter the eternal kingdom of God. Only when transformed into incorruptible, spiritual bodies can believers inherit the kingdom.

In 1 Corinthians 15:41-50, Paul continues to discuss the nature of resurrected bodies and the transformation that takes place in the resurrection. He draws parallels between celestial bodies and the transformation of human bodies in the resurrection, highlighting the diversity and glory of these new bodies. Paul distinguishes between natural and spiritual bodies, emphasizing that the resurrection will bring about a profound change from perishable, earthly bodies to imperishable, heavenly bodies. He also underscores the significance of bearing the image of Christ, the second Adam, and the necessity of transformation to inherit the kingdom of God.

Verse 51:

"Behold, I shew you a mystery; We shall not all sleep, but we shall all be changed."

Paul introduces a mystery—a divine truth previously hidden but now revealed. He explains that not all believers will experience physical death ("sleep"), for some will be alive when Christ returns.

However, all believers, whether living or deceased, will undergo a profound transformation.

Verse 52:

"In a moment, in the twinkling of an eye, at the last trump: for the trumpet shall sound, and the dead shall be raised incorruptible, and we shall be changed."

Paul describes the rapidity of the transformation. In an instant, at the sound of the final trumpet, the dead will be raised with incorruptible bodies, and the living will also experience a transformation. This trumpet call heralds the culmination of God's plan and the final resurrection.

Verse 53:

"For this corruptible must put on incorruption, and this mortal must put on immortality."

Paul clarifies the purpose of the transformation. Our corruptible, decaying bodies will be clothed with incorruption, and our mortal bodies will be clothed with immortality. This transformation is necessary for our eternal existence in the presence of God.

Verse 54:

"So, when this corruptible shall have put on incorruption, and this mortal shall have put on immortality, then shall be brought to pass the saying that is written, Death is swallowed up in victory."

Paul references Old Testament prophecies, particularly Isaiah 25:8. The transformation of our bodies marks the ultimate victory over death. It is a profound fulfillment of God's promise that death will be defeated.

Verse 55:

"O death, where is thy sting? O grave, where is thy victory?" Paul poetically expresses the triumph over death and the grave. The sting and victory that death once held are now nullified in light of the resurrection and eternal life.

Verse 56:

"The sting of death is sin, and the strength of sin is the law."

Paul explains the source of the sting of death—sin. Sin is transgression of the law, and the law reveals the power and extent of sin. However, through Christ's work, the power of sin is broken.

Verse 57:

"But thanks be to God, which giveth us the victory through our Lord Jesus Christ."

Paul expresses gratitude to God for granting believers the victory over death through the redemptive work of Jesus Christ. Victory is not achieved through human effort but is a gift from God.

Verse 58:

"Therefore, my beloved brethren, be ye steadfast, unmovable, always abounding in the work of the Lord, forasmuch as ye know that your labor is not in vain in the Lord."

Paul concludes by exhorting believers to stand firm and unwavering in their faith and service to the Lord. He encourages them to remain dedicated to the work of the Lord, knowing that their efforts have eternal significance and are not in vain.

In 1 Corinthians 15:51-58, Paul discusses the mystery of the transformation of believers at the return of Christ. He emphasizes the rapidity of this transformation, its purpose, and the victory over death it represents. Paul quotes Old Testament scriptures to highlight the defeat of death and sin through Christ. He offers gratitude to God for the gift of victory and encourages believers to stand firm and dedicated in their service to the Lord, knowing that their labor in the Lord is eternally meaningful.

Collection for the Saints and Final Instructions

The theme of 1 Corinthians chapter 16 is "Collection for the Saints and Final Instructions." In this chapter, the Apostle Paul provides instructions to the Corinthian church regarding a collection for the poor saints in Jerusalem and offers various final directives as he prepares to conclude his letter. The central theme revolves around the practical aspects of Christian giving and ministry, as well as Paul's personal requests and greetings. Here's an overview of the main themes and points in 1 Corinthians chapter 16:

1. The Collection for the Saints (1 Corinthians 16:1-4): Paul instructs the Corinthians to set aside a collection on the first day of the week for the poor saints in Jerusalem. He emphasizes the importance of this act of charity and the need for preparation to ensure that the gift is ready when he arrives.

2. Paul's Travel Plans (1 Corinthians 16:5-9): Paul discusses his travel plans, indicating that he intends to visit the Corinthians after his stay in Macedonia. He also mentions his desire to spend the winter with them in order to continue his ministry there.

3. Timothy and Apollos (1 Corinthians 16:10-12): Paul mentions the impending arrival of Timothy and encourages the Corinthians to welcome him. He also addresses the coming of Apollos and highlights the importance of treating these fellow workers in Christ with respect.

4. Final Exhortations and Greetings (1 Corinthians 16:13-24): Paul concludes his letter with a series of exhortations to the Corinthians, urging them to stand firm in the faith, be strong, and do everything in love. He sends greetings from various individuals, including Aquila and Priscilla, and concludes with a blessing of grace and love.

The central theme in 1 Corinthians chapter 16 is the practical aspects of Christian giving, ministry, and coordination within the church. Paul's instructions regarding the collection for the poor saints in Jerusalem exemplify the principle of caring for fellow believers in need. Additionally, he provides details on his travel plans and encourages the Corinthians to support and welcome fellow workers in the faith. The chapter serves as a reminder of the importance of both practical and spiritual aspects of Christian community life.

Verse 1:

"Now concerning the collection for the saints, as I have given order to the churches of Galatia, even so do ye."

Paul addresses the Corinthians regarding a collection for the saints, likely referring to a charitable offering for Christians in need. He instructs the Corinthians to follow the same directive he gave to the churches in Galatia, showing a unified approach to charity across the Christian community.

Verse 2:

"Upon the first day of the week, let every one of you lay by him in store, as God hath prospered him, that there be no gatherings when I come."

Paul specifies that this collection should take place on the first day of the week, which was likely the day of Christian gatherings (Sunday). He encourages each believer to set aside a portion of their income based on their prosperity, so that when he arrives, there won't be a need for last-minute gatherings or collections.

Verse 3:

"And when I come, whomsoever ye shall approve by your letters, them will I send to bring your liberality unto Jerusalem."

Paul plans to send representatives chosen and approved by the Corinthians, likely by written letters, to collect the charitable offerings and deliver them to the needy Christians in Jerusalem.

Verse 4:

"And if it be meet that I go also, they shall go with me."

Paul suggests that he might personally accompany the representatives to Jerusalem if the situation requires it. This demonstrates his commitment to the welfare of fellow believers.

Verse 5:

"Now I will come unto you when I shall pass through Macedonia, for I do pass through Macedonia."

Paul informs the Corinthians of his travel plans. He intends to visit them after passing through Macedonia, indicating a planned visit to their church.

Verse 6:

"And it may be that I will abide, yea, and winter with you, that ye may bring me on my journey whithersoever I go."

Paul expresses the possibility of staying with the Corinthians, even throughout the winter, and he hopes that they will assist him in continuing his journey to other destinations.

Verse 7:

"For I will not see you now by the way, but I trust to tarry a while with you if the Lord permit."

Paul acknowledges that he won't just pass by Corinth briefly, but he hopes to stay for an extended period, contingent upon the Lord's will.

Verse 8:

"But I will tarry at Ephesus until Pentecost."

Paul specifies that his current location is Ephesus, and he intends to remain there until the time of Pentecost. This suggests a commitment to the work in Ephesus before heading to Corinth.

Verse 9:

"For a great door and effectual is opened unto me, and there are many adversaries."

Paul mentions the opportunities for ministry in Ephesus but also acknowledges the presence of significant opposition. Despite challenges, he remains focused on the open doors for spreading the gospel.

Verse 10:

"Now if Timothy come, see that he may be with you without fear, for he worketh the work of the Lord as I also do."

Paul speaks highly of Timothy, his fellow worker in the ministry. He encourages the Corinthians to receive Timothy without fear, as he is dedicated to the work of the Lord, just as Paul is.

In 1 Corinthians 16:1-10, Paul addresses the Corinthians regarding a charitable collection for the saints. He provides instructions for this collection and his travel plans, emphasizing his intention to visit them and spend time with them. Paul also mentions the opportunities for ministry in Ephesus and encourages the Corinthians to receive Timothy without fear, as he is actively engaged in the work of the Lord. This passage demonstrates Paul's care for the well-being of fellow believers and his commitment to spreading the gospel.

Verse 11:

"Let no man therefore despise him: but conduct him forth in peace, that he may come unto me: for I look for him with the brethren."

Paul is instructing the Corinthians not to despise Timothy, who is likely coming to visit them. Instead, they should welcome him warmly and ensure he can come to Paul in peace. Paul eagerly anticipates Timothy's arrival along with other fellow believers.

Verse 12:

"As touching our brother Apollos, I greatly desired him to come unto you with the brethren, but his will was not at all to come at this time; but he will come when he shall have a convenient time."

Paul expresses his desire for Apollos, another fellow worker in the ministry, to visit the Corinthians, but Apollos has decided not to come at this time. However, he assures that Apollos will come when the time is right.

Verse 13:

"Watch ye, stand fast in the faith, quit you like men, be strong."

Paul encourages the Corinthians to remain vigilant and unwavering in their faith. He urges them to act with courage, strength, and determination in their Christian walk.

Verse 14:

"Let all your things be done with charity."

Paul emphasizes the importance of conducting their affairs with love (charity). Love should be the guiding principle in all their actions and decisions.

Verse 15:

"I beseech you, brethren (ye know the house of Stephanas, that it is the firstfruits of Achaia, and that they have addicted themselves to the ministry of the saints),"

Paul mentions the household of Stephanas, who were among the first converts in Achaia. They have devoted themselves to serving the needs of the saints, exemplifying a strong commitment to ministry.

Verse 16:

"That ye submit yourselves unto such, and to everyone that helpeth with us, and laboreth."

Paul encourages the Corinthians to honor and submit to individuals like Stephanas and anyone else who actively assists in the work of the ministry. Respect and support those who are dedicated to the service of fellow believers and the gospel.

Verse 17:

"I am glad of the coming of Stephanas and Fortunatus and Achaicus, for that which was lacking on your part, they have supplied."

Paul expresses his joy at the arrival of Stephanas, Fortunatus, and Achaicus, who have provided what was lacking from the Corinthians. They have come to support and serve, filling in the gaps in the Corinthians' service.

Verse 18:

"For they have refreshed my spirit and yours: therefore, acknowledge ye them that are such."

Paul highlights the mutual benefit of these brothers' service. They have not only refreshed his own spirit but have also contributed to the spiritual well-being of the Corinthians. He urges the Corinthians to recognize and appreciate individuals who are devoted to ministry. Verse 19:

"The churches of Asia salute you. Aquila and Priscilla salute you much in the Lord, with the church that is in their house."

Paul conveys greetings from the churches in Asia and from Aquila and Priscilla, a Christian couple who hosted a church in their house. These greetings serve to foster unity and fellowship among the Christian communities.

Verse 20:

"All the brethren greet you. Greet ye one another with a holy kiss."

Paul concludes by conveying greetings from all the fellow believers. He encourages the Corinthians to greet one another with a holy kiss, a customary sign of affection and fellowship in their culture.

In 1 Corinthians 16:11-20, Paul provides instructions regarding Timothy and Apollos and emphasizes the importance of love (charity) as the guiding principle in their actions. He commends the dedication of the household of Stephanas to the ministry of the saints and encourages the Corinthians to honor and support those actively involved in ministry. Paul also conveys greetings from various Christian communities and encourages the Corinthians to greet one another with affection and unity. This passage reflects the sense of community and shared commitment among early Christians.

Verse 21:

"The salutation of me, Paul, with mine own hand."

Paul personally adds this salutation in his own handwriting, a common practice in his letters. It serves to authenticate the letter's authorship and convey his personal greeting.

Verse 22:

"If any man loves not the Lord Jesus Christ, let him be Anathema, Maranatha."

Paul issues a serious declaration. Those who do not love the Lord Jesus Christ are to be "Anathema," which means accursed or devoted to destruction. "Maranatha" is an Aramaic phrase that means "Our Lord, come." It is a reminder of the impending return of Jesus Christ. Paul's message is clear: those who reject the love of Christ face a grave fate.

Verse 23:

"The grace of our Lord Jesus Christ be with you."

Paul concludes with a prayer for God's grace to be upon the Corinthians. It's a reminder of the importance of God's unmerited favor and help.

Verse 24:

"My love be with you all in Christ Jesus. Amen."

Paul expresses his love for the Corinthians and emphasizes that this love is rooted in their shared faith in Christ Jesus. He closes the letter with the customary "Amen," signifying affirmation and conclusion.

In 1 Corinthians 16:21-24, Paul adds a personal salutation in his own handwriting and conveys a powerful message about the importance of loving the Lord Jesus Christ. He emphasizes the impending return of Christ and prays for God's grace to be upon the Corinthians. Paul concludes with a declaration of his love for them in Christ Jesus and affirms the message with "Amen." This closing passage underscores the significance of love, faith, and the hope of Christ's return in the life of a believer.

CONCLUSION

The conclusion of the First Corinthians wraps up the letter by summarizing key points and reiterating the themes and principles that the Apostle Paul has addressed throughout the letter.

In his first letter to the Corinthians, Paul has covered a wide range of topics and issues facing the church in Corinth. He has provided practical guidance on matters of morality, discipline, unity, and the proper use of spiritual gifts. The central theme throughout the letter has been the call to live according to the wisdom and principles of Christ, rather than worldly wisdom or human divisions.

Paul's emphasis on the importance of love as the greatest virtue and the need for unity and cooperation among believers serves as a unifying thread throughout the letter. He calls for believers to seek the welfare of others, avoid causing others to stumble, and prioritize the building up of the body of Christ.

The central message of 1 Corinthians is the call to live as a community of believers, committed to the principles of love, selflessness, and unity. Paul's teaching on the resurrection of the dead and the future hope of believers is a foundational element of the Christian faith, providing assurance and encouragement to face life's challenges.

In conclusion, 1 Corinthians offers timeless wisdom for Christian living. It calls believers to exemplify the love and unity of Christ, to build up one another, and to keep their focus on the hope of the resurrection. As the Corinthians faced various issues and disputes, Paul's letter remains a valuable source of guidance for believers in any age, reminding us to live according to the wisdom and principles of Christ, with love and unity as our guiding principles.

www.ingramcontent.com/pod-product-compliance
Lightning Source LLC
Chambersburg PA
CBHW061258120726
48001CB00001B/362